JAMESTOWN  EDUCATION

The Outer Edge™
Friend or Foe?

Henry Billings

Melissa Billings

 Glencoe

New York, New York   Columbus, Ohio   Chicago, Illinois   Peoria, Illinois   Woodland Hills, California

Reviewers

Kati Pearson
Literacy Coordinator
Carver Middle School
4500 West Columbia Street
Orlando, FL 32811

Suzanne Zweig
Reading Specialist
Sullivan High School
6631 North Bosworth Avenue
Chicago, IL 60626

Beth Dalton
Reading Consultant
Los Angeles County Office
  of Education
9300 Imperial Avenue
Downey, CA 90240

Susan Jones
Reading Specialist
Hastings High School
12301 High Star
Houston, Texas 77072

Glencoe

The *McGraw-Hill* Companies

ISBN: 0-07-869054-4

Send all queries to:
Glencoe/McGraw-Hill
8787 Orion Place
Columbus, OH 43240-4027

1 2 3 4 5 6 7 8 9   024   10 09 08 07 06 05 04

Contents

Unit Three

To the Student

Some animals are our friends. They are wonderful companions and even protect us at times. Other animals are our foes. They fear us and will attack us if they feel we are a threat to them. There are 13 true stories in this book. In them you will learn about some animals who have done brave deeds and others who are a serious threat to our safety.

As you do the lessons in this book, you will improve your reading skills. This will help you increase your reading comprehension. You will also improve your thinking skills. The lessons include types of questions often found on state and national tests. Working with these questions will help you prepare for tests you may have to take in the future.

How to Use This Book

About the Book. *Friend or Foe?* has three units. Each one has four lessons. Each lesson starts with a true story. The stories are about animals who are our friends and animals who are our enemies. Each story is followed by a group of seven exercises. They test comprehension and thinking skills. They will help you understand and think about what you read. At the end of the lesson, you can give your personal response. You can also rate how well you understood what you read.

The Sample Lesson The first lesson in the book is a sample. It explains how to complete the questions. It also shows how to score your answers. The correct answers are printed in lighter type. In some cases, the reasons an answer is correct are given. Studying these reasons will help you learn how to think through the questions. You might have questions about how to do the exercises or score them. If so, you should ask those questions now, before you start Unit One.

Working Through Each Lesson. Start each lesson by looking at the photo. Next read the caption. Before you read the story, guess what you think it will be about. Then read the story.

After you finish the story, do the exercises. Study the directions for each exercise. They will tell you how to mark your answers. Do all seven exercises. Then check your work. Your teacher will give you an answer key to do this. Follow the directions after each exercise to find your score. At the end of the lesson, add up your total score. Record that score on the graph on page 115.

At the end of each unit, you will complete a Compare and Contrast Chart. The chart will help you see what some of the stories in that unit have in common. It will also help you explore your own ideas about the events in the stories.

Sample Lesson

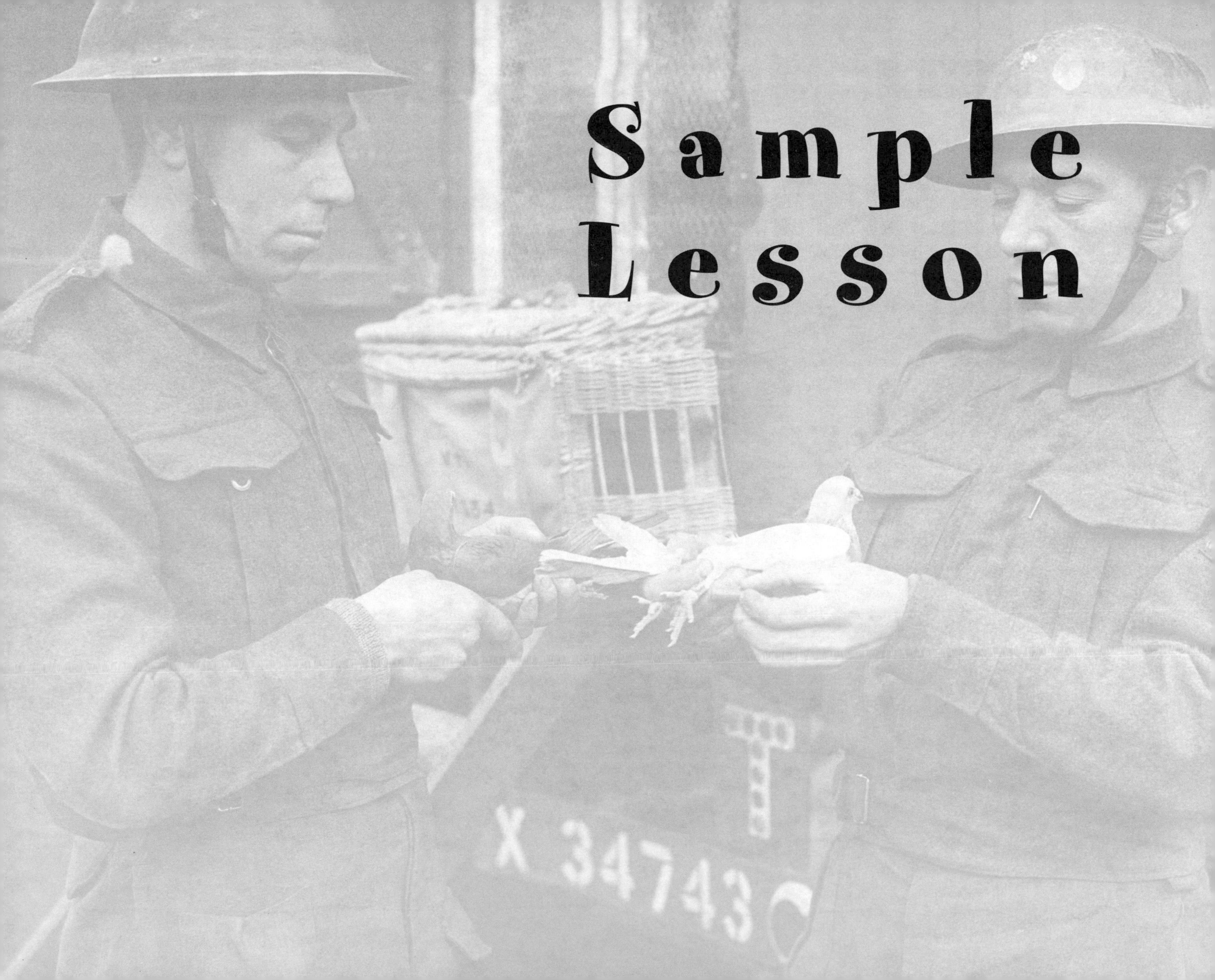

Birds at War

The plane plummeted into the North Atlantic Ocean. The three men on board fell into the cold sea. They climbed onto a small boat, and then they looked around. They were in big trouble. They were far from land, and they had no food or water. Worse, they had no way to keep warm. Unless someone came to save them, they would die.

2 The men had to get help—fast. But how? The year was 1942. It was during World War II. The men were British soldiers. If they could get a message to other soldiers, they might be saved. But the men had only one hope of doing that. Their hope lay with a carrier pigeon.

3 A carrier pigeon is a special kind of bird. No matter where it is taken, it will always fly to its home. Because of this, it is also called a homing pigeon. No one knows how these birds find their way. But they can fly hundreds of miles and not get lost.

4 During World War I and World War II, many soldiers used these birds. At times it was the only way to send a

---

Shown here are soldiers with carrier pigeons used in World War II.

message. A soldier would write a note on a piece of paper. He would put it in a tiny box. He would tie the box to the bird's leg. Then he would toss the bird into the air to fly home.

5 The three British soldiers had a carrier pigeon with them in their plane. After they crashed, they looked for her. It took a while, but at last they found her. Oil from the plane had gotten on her feathers. But she was alive.

6 The men took her from her cage. They tossed her into the air and hoped for the best. Night was falling. Still, the bird flew without stopping. On and on she went. After more than 100 miles, she came to an air force camp in Norway. This was her home. She was wet, tired, and still covered with oil, but she had made it.

7 Soldiers at the air force camp knew how fast a carrier pigeon flies. They added in the speed of the wind. That helped them figure out where the plane went down. They rushed to the men in the boat and saved them.

8 The British soldiers were fine. The pigeon, too, was okay. Her eyes, however, had been hurt. Her long, hard trip had worn her out. From then on, she blinked slowly. It looked almost like she was winking. Before the trip, she had not had a name. Now she was called "Winkie." The men she had saved threw a party for her. Later Winkie was given the Dickin Medal. This is England's top military prize for animals.

9 Not all carrier pigeons were so lucky. Some of them were shot down by enemy soldiers. The enemy also trained larger birds to attack and kill the pigeons. Still, some got through. They became heroes. One was a World War I pigeon named Cher Ami. *Cher ami* means "dear friend" in French.

10 Cher Ami flew 12 times. In one trip he saved nearly 200 men. It happened in 1918. A group of 500 soldiers in the U.S. army got trapped between two hills. The enemy was all around them. A battle began. Many Americans died on the first day. By the second day, there were only about 200 left. They feared they would soon be killed as well.

11 Then help came—or so they thought. Other Americans got close to the hills. They began to shoot. They thought they were firing at the enemy. But, in fact, they were hitting the trapped Americans. If they didn't stop firing, they would kill them all. Charles Whittlesey was in charge of the trapped men. He wanted to send a message to the men who were shooting. He sent out one pigeon after another, but none made it. Each one was shot down. At last, he had just one pigeon left—Cher Ami.

12 Whittlesey tied a message to Cher Ami's leg. The message told where his men were. It told how the shots were hitting them. It asked that the firing stop.

13 Whittlesey tossed Cher Ami into the air. After that, there was nothing more Whittlesey could do. The enemy saw the pigeon flying away. They opened fire. Many men shot at the bird, but they all missed him. Soon Cher Ami was far away. He flew as fast as he could. After 25 miles, he reached his home. The message got through. The guns were turned toward the enemy. Whittlesey and his men were saved.

14 On his last trip, Cher Ami was hurt. He lost sight in one eye. He also lost his left leg. By then he was a great hero. One of the men he had saved made a tiny wooden leg for him. Another man wrote a poem about him.

15 Today most people have never heard of Cher Ami or Winkie. But these birds helped win wars and save lives. They gave a whole new meaning to the words "fine-feathered friends."

A Finding the Main Idea

One statement below tells the main idea of the article. One statement is too general, or too broad. The other statement explains only part of the article; it is too narrow. Label the statements using the following key:

M—Main Idea   B—Too Broad   N—Too Narrow

B   1. People call many animals friends. [This statement is true, but it is *too broad.* It does not tell why some animals are called friends.]

M   2. Carrier pigeons saved the lives of many soldiers during World War I and World War II. [This statement is the *main idea.* It tells you that the article is about pigeons that did an important job during times of war.]

N   3. Most people have never heard of the carrier pigeons Cher Ami and Winkie. [This statement is true, but it is *too narrow.* It gives only a few facts from the article.]

Score 4 points for each correct answer.

_____ **Total Score:** Finding the Main Idea

B Recalling Facts

How well do you remember the facts in the article? Put an X in the box next to the answer that correctly completes each statement.

1. Carrier pigeons, also called homing pigeons, are special because they
   - ☐ a. can be raised in people's homes.
   - ☒ b. always find their way home.
   - ☐ c. make their own homes.

2. Soldiers in World War I and World War II used carrier pigeons
   - ☒ a. to carry messages.
   - ☐ b. as food along the way.
   - ☐ c. to help lost soldiers find their way home.

3. After some British soldiers crashed in the North Atlantic Ocean, their carrier pigeon flew
   - ☐ a. all the way to America.
   - ☐ b. 1,000 miles to France.
   - ☒ c. 100 miles to Norway.

4. On his last trip, Cher Ami
   - ☐ a. was killed.
   - ☒ b. got hurt.
   - ☐ c. forgot his way home.

Score 4 points for each correct answer.

_____ **Total Score:** Recalling Facts

C Making Inferences

When you draw a conclusion that is not directly stated in the text, you are making an inference. Put an X in the box next to the statement that is a correct inference.

1.

☐ a. Carrier pigeons will fly anywhere their owners ask them to go.

☐ b. Carrier pigeons are so fast that no other bird can catch them.

☒ c. Carrier pigeons can fly well even with things tied to their legs.

2.

☒ a. It is hard to shoot a bird that is flying away from you.

☐ b. Carrier pigeons cannot find their way home at night.

☐ c. During World War I, there was no way to get in touch with people except by carrier pigeon.

Score 4 points for each correct answer.

_____ **Total Score:** Making Inferences

D Using Words

Put an X in the box next to the definition below that is closest in meaning to the underlined word.

1. When the girl threw the doll out the window, it plummeted to the ground below.

☒ a. fell

☐ b. floated

☐ c. flew

2. The soldiers fought bravely.

☐ a. large birds trained to carry messages

☒ b. people paid to fight

☐ c. planes that flew during World War II

3. The pigeon rose into the air when it heard the loud noise.

☐ a. plane

☐ b. kite

☒ c. bird

4. Bees attack anyone who hurts their hive.

☒ a. come after and try to hurt

☐ b. run away from

☐ c. make friends with

5. We all thanked the <u>heroes</u> for saving the children who fell in the lake.

☐ a. smart people who know a lot

☒ b. brave people who do good things

☐ c. funny people who tell jokes

6. In the <u>army</u>, my uncle learned how to shoot a gun.

☐ a. a school that teaches people how to save lives

☐ b. a marching band

☒ c. a large group of people trained to fight

Score 4 points for each correct answer.

_____ **Total Score:** Using Words

E | Author's Approach

Put an X in the box next to the correct answer.

1. The main purpose of the first paragraph is to

☐ a. tell how brave carrier pigeons are.

☒ b. show how much trouble the soldiers were in.

☐ c. make readers want to visit the North Atlantic Ocean.

2. From the statements below, choose the one that you believe the author would agree with.

☒ a. Carrier pigeons are amazing animals.

☐ b. Carrier pigeons are not worth much.

☐ c. No one remembers anymore what carrier pigeons did during World War I and World War II.

3. What purpose does the author give in paragraph 15 for writing the article?

☐ a. The author wants readers to know that Cher Ami and Winkie are now dead.

☐ b. The author wants readers to know that carrier pigeons have fine feathers.

☒ c. The author wants readers to know that carrier pigeons saved lives.

Score 4 points for each correct answer.

_____ **Total Score:** Author's Approach

F Summarizing and Paraphrasing

Put an X in the box next to the correct answer.

1. Which summary says all the important things about the article?

   ☐ a. Cher Ami was a carrier pigeon. During World War I, many people thought Cher Ami was a hero. [This summary gives some small details from the article but misses too many important ones.]

   ☒ b. During World Wars I and II, carrier pigeons helped soldiers by carrying messages. Two of those pigeons, Cher Ami and Winkie, saved men's lives. [This summary says all the most important things.]

   ☐ c. A carrier pigeon named Winkie started blinking after a 100-mile flight. The flight must have been hard on the bird. [This summary gives some small details from the article but misses too many important ones.]

2. Which sentence means the same as the following one? "They tossed her into the air and hoped for the best."

   ☐ a. They hoped that the pigeon knew how to fly.

   ☐ b. After the pigeon flew away, they said that she was their best friend.

   ☒ c. They let the pigeon go and hoped that she would get them help. [The sentence replaces *hoped for the best* with a phrase that means the same thing.]

G Critical Thinking

Put an X in the box next to the correct answer.

1. Choose the statement below that states an opinion.

   ☐ a. A carrier pigeon named Winkie got the Dickin Medal.

   ☐ b. Cher Ami helped save the lives of about 200 soldiers.

   ☒ c. Carrier pigeons are the best animals.

2. Winkie and Cher Ami are alike because

   ☐ a. both helped soldiers in World War I.

   ☒ b. both carried important messages.

   ☐ c. both came from France.

3. How is the carrier pigeon an example of a friend?

   ☒ a. Carrier pigeons have helped people.

   ☐ b. Carrier pigeons can fly for a long time.

   ☐ c. Carrier pigeons always fly home.

4. What was the effect of Winkie's long, hard trip?

   ☐ a. The bird got the name Cher Ami.

   ☒ b. The bird started blinking slowly.

   ☐ c. Someone wrote a poem about the bird.

Score 4 points for each correct answer.

_____ **Total Score:** Summarizing and Paraphrasing

5. In which paragraph did you find the information or details to answer question 4?

☐ a. paragraph 6

☐ b. paragraph 7

☒ c. paragraph 8

Score 4 points for each correct answer.

_____ **Total Score:** Critical Thinking

Enter your score for each activity. Add the scores together. Record your total score on the graph on page 115.

_____ Finding the Main Idea

_____ Recalling Facts

_____ Making Inferences

_____ Using Words

_____ Author's Approach

_____ Summarizing and Paraphrasing

_____ Critical Thinking

_____ **Total Score**

Personal Response

What new question do you have about this topic? [Write down one question that came into your mind as you read the article.]

_____

_____

Self-Assessment

From reading this article, I have learned _____

_____

_____

[Think of facts or ideas that you learned from the article.]

Self-Assessment

You can take charge of your own progress. Here are some features to help you focus on your progress in learning reading and thinking skills.

Personal Response and Self-Assessment. These questions help you connect the stories to your life. They help you think about your understanding of what you have read.

Comprehension and Critical Thinking Progress Graph. A graph at the end of the book helps you to keep track of your progress. Check the graph often with your teacher. Together, decide whether you need more work on some skills. What types of skills cause you trouble? Talk with your teacher about ways to work on these.

A sample Progress Graph is shown on the right. The first three lessons have been filled in to show you how to use the graph.

Comprehension and Critical Thinking Progress Graph

Directions: Write your score for each lesson in the box under the number of the lesson. Then put a small X on the line directly above the number of the lesson and across from the score you earned. Chart your progress by drawing a line to connect the Xs.

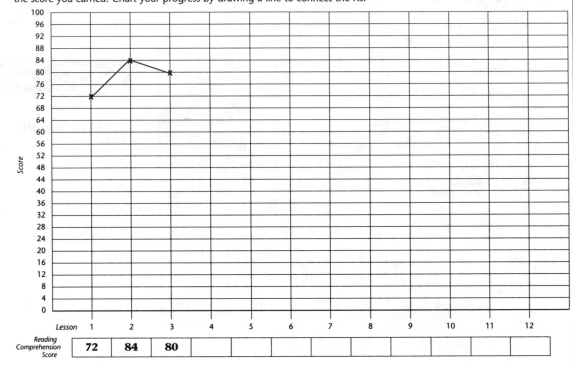

Reading Comprehension Score	72	84	80									

UNIT ONE

The Most Dangerous Animal in Africa

They're big. They're fast. And when hippos get mad, they don't mess around. In fact, each year more people are killed by hippos than any other animal in Africa.

2   In 2003 one of these people was Ester Jobe. Jobe sneaked into a wildlife park in South Africa. She and two friends wanted to catch some fish. Jobe walked into the water with her fish basket. As she did so, she came upon a hippo. It had been resting in the water. Hippos often do this. They have no hair covering their bodies. If they spent much time in the hot sun, their skin would crack and burn. So during the day, they are most often found in the water.

3   Jobe did not know that she was walking toward a hippopotamus. She thought it was a big fish. By the time she saw she was wrong, it was too late. The hippo attacked. Hippos do not eat meat. Mostly they just eat grass. But in the front of their mouths they have four huge teeth. These are very long and very sharp. Each

Pictured here is an adult hippopotamus similar to the ones described in this story.

one is about two feet long. These teeth are so sharp they can cut through the skin of a crocodile. When the hippo sank its teeth into Ester Jobe, she didn't stand much of a chance.

4   People felt terrible that Jobe had died. But what happened to her proved one thing. No one should wander through a wildlife park. After all, wild animals live there. If they feel threatened, they may fight. Jobe did not mean to hurt the hippo. But the hippo could not read her mind. All it knew was that another animal was coming closer and closer. To save itself, it attacked.

5   The same sort of thing happened to Annatjie Mienie in 2002. Like Jobe, Mienie was in a wildlife park. But Mienie did not sneak in. South Africa lets people stay at certain spots in the park. Mienie was at one of these places. She was standing near the water. She was taking pictures of a crocodile. Then she saw a baby hippo. Mienie hoped to get a shot of it too. She turned toward the baby. At that point, the baby's mother got mad. The mother thought Mienie might hurt the baby. So it charged. It opened its four-foot-wide mouth. Again and again it bit Mienie. By the time it stopped, Mienie's life was ending.

6   People also cross paths with hippos outside of wildlife parks. People need water, and so do hippos. Often both groups meet up at the same watering hole.

In the past, there were fewer people in Africa. There were more watering holes too. Now people have taken much of the land where hippos live. So hippos and humans keep bumping into each other. When they do, humans may make the wrong move. They may get too close to its baby. Or they may step between a hippo and its watering hole.

7   William Mbazima knew that hippos lived in the river near his South African home. But he went there anyway. He had to go. He had to catch fish to feed his family. For 29 years, he was lucky. He saw lots of hippos in the water. But none ever attacked him. Then, when he was 78 years old, his luck ran out. On August 24, 2001, Mbazima set out for the river. He cut a path through the high grass near the shore. But as he did so, he came to a hippo and its baby.

8   "In the wink of an eye, a hippo stormed me," Mbazima said.

9   The hippo caught Mbazima in its mouth. Its teeth cut through his chest.

10   "I can't remember much after the attack," he said.

11   When the hippo let Mbazima go, he was still alive. Other fishermen ran to help him. But five hours passed before they could get him to the hospital. Somehow his heart kept beating. At the hospital, doctors worked hard to save him. They did it. Mbazima spent a long time in the hospital. But he lived. He knew it had been a close call. He did not want to get near hippos ever again. But he knew he would go back to fishing at the river again.

12   "Hunger and poverty will drive me back there," he said.

13   Mbazima still hoped to live side by side with hippos. But not everyone is willing to live and let live when it comes to hippos. In 2002 a hippo came near a South African village. It was looking for food and water. The people in the village wanted it to go away. For three days they threw stones at it. At last the hippo had had enough. It turned and ran toward a woman. The woman lived, but she was badly hurt.

14   Then there are people who try to kill hippos. This is against the law. But people do it anyway. Some want hippo meat. Some want to sell the animals' teeth. In 2002 a man went after a hippo. He hoped to kill it. But his plan didn't work. The hippo attacked him instead. Like so many others, he learned why the hippo is called the most dangerous animal in Africa.

A | Finding the Main Idea

One statement below tells the main idea of the article. One statement is too general, or too broad. The other statement explains only part of the article; it is too narrow. Label the statements using the following key:

M—Main Idea   B—Too Broad   N—Too Narrow

_N_ 1. Ester Jobe didn't know that she had come upon a hippo until it had already started its attack.

_B_ 2. People must understand that even wild animals that live in a wildlife park can and do attack humans.

_M_ 3. Many attacks on humans by hippos have proved that the hippo is a very dangerous animal.

Score 4 points for each correct answer.

_____ **Total Score:** Finding the Main Idea

B | Recalling Facts

How well do you remember the facts in the article? Put an X in the box next to the answer that correctly completes each statement.

1. The favorite food of hippos is
☒ a. grass.
☐ b. small animals.
☐ c. humans.

2. Annatjie Mienie was attacked by a hippo when she was
☐ a. trying to kill a baby hippo.
☒ b. taking pictures of a baby hippo.
☐ c. sneaking into a wildlife park.

3. William Mbazima went to the river near his home to
☐ a. take pictures of a hippo.
☐ b. kill a hippo.
☒ c. catch fish to feed his family.

4. After people in a South African village threw stones at a hippo for three days, the hippo
☒ a. attacked a woman.
☐ b. was scared away.
☐ c. knocked down their houses.

Score 4 points for each correct answer.

_____ **Total Score:** Recalling Facts

C Making Inferences

When you draw a conclusion that is not directly stated in the text, you are making an inference. Put an X in the box next to the statement that is a correct inference.

1.

☒ a. Most people in South Africa think that surprising a hippo would be fun.

☐ b. Hippos spend their days in the water so they can eat all the fish they want.

☒ c. Hippos will do almost anything to keep their babies safe.

2.

☐ a. The only thing that will make a hippo attack is if someone comes between it and its baby.

☐ b. Hippos can move very quickly.

☒ c. If a hippo attacks you, you will surely be killed.

Score 4 points for each correct answer.

_____ **Total Score:** Making Inferences

D Using Words

Put an X in the box next to the definition below that is closest in meaning to the underlined word or phrase.

1. Paula put up a <u>wildlife</u> poster from the zoo on her bedroom wall.

☐ a. pretty pictures

☒ b. wild animals

☐ c. a lot of money

2. When our dog feels <u>threatened</u>, it growls and bares its teeth.

☒ a. tired and sleepy

☐ b. happy and friendly

☒ c. in trouble and not safe

3. <u>Humans</u> need water, just as hippos do.

☒ a. people

☒ b. animals that are dying out

☐ c. young hippos

4. The girl who had been lost in the woods had just enough water to stay <u>alive</u> for two days.

☐ a. dead

☐ b. old

☒ c. living

5. People who live in <u>poverty</u> may not have enough food or a safe place to live.

☐ a. the state of being poor
☒ b. the state of being young
☐ c. the state of being happy

6. We were warned that the trip down the river was <u>dangerous</u>.

☐ a. boring
☒ b. full of risk
☐ c. fun

Score 4 points for each correct answer.

_____ **Total Score:** Using Words

E | **Author's Approach**

Put an X in the box next to the correct answer.

1. The main purpose of the first paragraph is to

☐ a. explain why hippos attack humans.
☐ b. tell why people should be kind to hippos.
☒ c. tell what hippos look like and how they act.

2. From the statements below, choose the one that you believe the author would agree with.

☐ a. Hippos would make good pets.
☐ b. You should stay away from wild hippos.
☒ c. Hippos are bigger and faster than any other animal.

3. Choose the statement below that best describes the author's opinion in paragraph 4.

☒ a. People should not be surprised that hippos attack when they are afraid.
☐ b. All wildlife parks should be closed because they are too scary.
☐ c. Hippos are smarter than people.

Score 4 points for each correct answer

_____ **Total Score:** Author's Approach

F | Summarizing and Paraphrasing

Put an X in the box next to the correct answer.

1. Which summary says all the important things about the article?

- ☐ a. In 2002 a man in Africa wanted to kill a hippo for its meat and teeth. He was ready to kill the hippo. Instead, the hippo attacked and killed the man.
- ☒ b. African hippos have attacked many people, including a woman looking for fish, a woman taking a picture of a hippo baby, a man fishing, a woman at a village, and a hunter.
- ☐ c. No one knows exactly how a wild animal will act. The best way to stay safe is to keep far away from wild animals, such as hippos.

2. Which sentence means the same thing as the following sentence? "He knew it had been a close call."

- ☐ a. He knew he had come close to dying.
- ☒ b. He knew how to call a hippo to make it come close.
- ☐ c. He knew that the hippo had come very close to him.

Score 4 points for each correct answer.

_____ **Total Score:** Summarizing and Paraphrasing

G | Critical Thinking

Put an X in the box next to the correct answer.

1. Choose the statement below that states a fact.
- ☐ a. Hippos are the scariest animals in the world.
- ☒ b. The hippo has four two-foot-long teeth.
- ☐ c. I don't like hippos enough to want to save them.

2. From information in the article, you can predict that
- ☒ a. hippos will keep attacking people if they feel threatened.
- ☐ b. hippos will learn that they should not attack people.
- ☐ c. hippos will scare people so much that no one will ever come near one again.

3. Hippos and humans are alike because
- ☒ a. they both have no hair covering their bodies.
- ☐ b. they both have teeth sharp enough to cut through a crocodile's skin.
- ☐ c. they both need water to live.

4. What was the cause of the hippo's attack on Annatjie Mienie?
- ☒ a. The hippo wanted to eat Mienie.
- ☐ b. The hippo thought Mienie might hurt its baby.
- ☐ c. Mienie had come between the hippo and the watering hole.

5. In which paragraph did you find the information or
   details to answer question 4?

   ☐ a. paragraph 5
   ☐ b. paragraph 7
   ☐ c. paragraph 14

Score 4 points for each correct answer.

_____ **Total Score:** Critical Thinking

Enter your score for each activity. Add the scores
together. Record your total score on the graph on
page 115.

_____ Finding the Main Idea

_____ Recalling Facts

_____ Making Inferences

_____ Using Words

_____ Author's Approach

_____ Summarizing and Paraphrasing

_____ Critical Thinking

_____ **Total Score**

Personal Response

What was most surprising or interesting to you about this
article?

_____

_____

Self-Assessment

I can't really understand how _____

_____

When Bulls Go Bananas

"You never want to turn your back on a bull."

2 That's what New York farmer Hugh Henderson says. Henderson has a point. Each year, farmers are killed when their bulls go wild without warning.

3 No one knows why bulls do this. They may be perfectly quiet one minute. But they might try to kill you the next.

4 "You just can't trust them," says Henderson. "I think it's just their nature."

5 Most farmers have no problem with their bulls. But when a bull does act up, it means trouble. Just ask the Mills family of Michigan. On March 3, 2002, 13-year-old Andrew Mills was working on the family farm. Suddenly a bull came after him. It knocked him off his feet. He was not badly hurt. But the bull then attacked his father, Mark. The bull knocked Mark to the ground. It stepped on him. Bulls weigh about 1,500 pounds. They can kill people just by standing on them.

6 Fifteen-year-old Kate Mills saw what was happening.

The bull pictured here looks like it is about to attack the photographer. Attacks by bulls is the subject of this selection.

She knew the bull would kill her father unless she acted quickly. Jumping on the tractor, Kate drove straight toward the bull. After she hit the bull on its side, it moved away from her father. Andrew picked up a board that was lying nearby. He waved it at the bull. Together, Kate and Andrew held off the bull as best they could.

7 Two rescue workers came. But they could not get to Mark. The bull was in their way. They sent out a call. They asked for help "from anyone, from anywhere." More people came. These people chased the bull off so the rescue workers could get to Mark. Mark was rushed to the hospital. He was in bad shape. But thanks to his children, he was alive.

8 The Mills family did not have any warning that their bull would attack. Neither did New Zealand farmer Bruce Dustow. One day Dustow wanted to do some work on a fence. He got some wood and carried it across a field. Dustow kept a bull in the field. But that didn't worry him. The bull had never been a problem. In fact, Dustow thought of it as his pet.

9 On this day, however, the bull was not feeling friendly. It came up behind Dustow. The bull knocked him to the ground. It dug into him with its horns. Then it lifted its head and tossed him into the air. Some of Dustow's workers ran to get help, but by then it was too late. Dustow died in the field.

10   Sometimes bulls do give signals that they are ready to snap. British farmer David Mytum got a signal. He and his wife, Susan, thought their bull was safe to be around. Often they went out to the field and petted it. They let their children do the same. But on July 9, 2002, the bull seemed angry. When David came out to it, it knocked him down.

11   Susan was nearby. She saw David curled up on the ground near the bull. She ran over. She hit the bull with a stick until it moved away. David was not badly hurt. But the Mytums knew they could no longer trust their bull. They made plans to get rid of it. David said that he would carry a stick with him until the bull was gone.

12   Just two days later, though, he forgot. When he went into the field, he did not take a stick. His hands were empty. Again the bull attacked him. This time Susan was not there to save him. The bull killed him.

13   Vermont farmer Floyd Stone did not have as much warning as David Mytum. In fact, he did not really have a warning at all. But he did have a "funny feeling." That was what he called it. Stone went to the barn one morning. He planned to move his bull out to a field. He took hold of the ring in its nose and began to lead it out the barn door. Stone had owned this bull for years. It had never given him any trouble. But on this day, Stone sensed that something was not right. So before he left the barn, he grabbed a pitchfork. A pitchfork is a tool that looks like a big fork. Farmers use it to throw hay or to break ground. Taking the pitchfork saved Stone's life.

14   Once outside, the bull suddenly went wild. It shook its head back and forth. Stone lost his grip on the nose ring. The bull then charged at Stone and knocked him down. It hit him with its horns and kicked at him with its feet.

15   Luckily, a neighbor passed by just at this moment. The man saw Stone on the ground. He also saw the pitchfork, which Stone had dropped. The neighbor grabbed the pitchfork and used it to drive the bull away.

16   Stone lived through the attack. Like David Mytum, he said he would never trust a bull again. But while Mytum soon forgot his words, Floyd Stone has always remembered. From that day on, he has carried a stick or pitchfork whenever he has gone near a bull. ✖

A | Finding the Main Idea

One statement below tells the main idea of the article. One statement is too general, or too broad. The other statement explains only part of the article; it is too narrow. Label the statements using the following key:

M—Main Idea   B—Too Broad   N—Too Narrow

_M_ 1. A bull that went wild knocked Mark Mills down and stepped on him, almost killing him.

_B_ 2. It is not wise to think you are safe around some animals.

_N_ 3. Bulls that seem tame can go wild at times and hurt people.

Score 4 points for each correct answer.

_____ **Total Score:** Finding the Main Idea

B | Recalling Facts

How well do you remember the facts in the article? Put an X in the box next to the answer that correctly completes each statement.

1. After Mark Mills was attacked by a bull, his daughter
   - ☐ a. beat the bull off with a stick.
   - ☒ b. ran a tractor into the bull.
   - ☐ c. was able to do nothing but call for help.

2. Bruce Dustow was a farmer in
   - ☐ a. New Zealand.
   - ☒ b. New Hampshire.
   - ☐ c. Michigan.

3. After David Mytum was attacked by his bull, he
   - ☒ a. killed it.
   - ☐ b. sold it right away.
   - ☐ c. made plans to get rid of it.

4. Floyd Stone's neighbor saw a bull attacking Stone. He grabbed Stone's pitchfork and
   - ☐ a. drove the wild bull away with it.
   - ☐ b. stabbed and killed the wild bull with it.
   - ☐ c. ran away with it.

Score 4 points for each correct answer.

_4_ **Total Score:** Recalling Facts

C Making Inferences

When you draw a conclusion that is not directly stated in the text, you are making an inference. Put an X in the box next to the statement that is a correct inference.

1.

☒ a. Bulls are very strong animals.

☐ b. Bulls are always afraid of people.

☐ c. Bulls make good pets.

2.

☐ a. If the farmers had been kind to the bulls, the bulls would not have gone wild.

☒ b. One way to pull a bull is by the ring in its nose.

☐ c. A bull will attack only when someone has hurt it.

Score 4 points for each correct answer.

_____6_____ **Total Score:** Making Inferences

D Using Words

Put an X in the box next to the definition below that is closest in meaning to the underlined word.

1. It is my cat's <u>nature</u> to sleep a lot during the day.

☒ a. the sound that a cat makes

☐ b. the way something is from the start

☐ c. soft fur

2. Both of my brothers <u>weigh</u> too much to sit in that little chair anymore.

☒ a. are loud

☐ b. are angry

☐ c. are a certain number of pounds

3. People clapped when the <u>rescue</u> team carried the baby from the burning house.

☐ a. saving

☐ b. hurting

☐ c. laughing

4. The sound of thunder far away is a <u>warning</u> that a storm will soon be here.

☐ a. a sign that something bad is coming

☐ b. a story about something scary

☐ c. a day on which something bad happens

5. He lost his <u>grip</u>, and so he fell off the climbing bars.

☒ a. bike

☐ b. dog

☐ c. hold

6. Maybe a loud noise will <u>drive</u> those hungry birds away from the garden.

☐ a. play

☒ b. chase

☐ c. look

Score 4 points for each correct answer.

___2___ **Total Score:** Using Words

E Author's Approach

Put an X in the box next to the correct answer.

1. The author uses the first sentence of the article to

☐ a. tell the reader what the article will be about.

☒ b. tell why farmers do not trust bulls.

☐ c. show how bulls and other animals are different.

2. Choose the statement below that is the weakest argument for being afraid of a bull.

☐ a. Some bulls go wild at times.

☒ b. A wild bull can hurt people.

☐ c. Most bulls are quiet and good.

3. The author tells this story mainly by

☒ a. making up short stories about different kinds of animals.

☐ b. showing what happened to different people.

☐ c. showing what happened to one person.

Score 4 points for each correct answer.

___3___ **Total Score:** Author's Approach

F | Summarizing and Paraphrasing

Put an X in the box next to the correct answer.

1. Which summary says all the important things about the article?

☒ a. Vermont farmer Floyd Stone could tell that something was wrong with his bull, so he kept a pitchfork near him. When his bull went wild, his neighbor fought the bull with the pitchfork.

☐ b. When a bull goes wild, it is very hard to stop. Even when many people are fighting it, the bull may win. A bull weighs about 1,500 pounds.

☐ c. A Michigan farmer was attacked by his bull. He was hurt but lived. A farmer in New Zealand and a British farmer were killed by bulls that went wild. A Vermont farmer was saved from his bull by a neighbor.

2. Which sentence means the same thing as the following sentence? "Stone lost his grip on the nose ring."

☐ a. Stone lost the key to the nose ring.

☒ b. Stone had to let go of the nose ring.

☐ c. Stone pulled the nose ring off the bull.

Score 4 points for each correct answer.

___6___ **Total Score:** Summarizing and Paraphrasing

G | Critical Thinking

Put an X in the box next to the correct answer.

1. Choose the statement below that states a fact.

☐ a. All bulls are mean animals.

☐ b. Bulls weigh about 1,500 pounds.

☐ c. It is never a good idea to raise a bull.

2. From information in the article, you can predict that

☐ a. Floyd Stone will thank his neighbor for helping him.

☒ b. someday Floyd Stone will start to trust bulls again.

☐ c. Floyd Stone will hate bulls for the rest of his life.

3. David Mytum and Floyd Stone are different because

☒ a. Mytum was killed by a bull, but Stone lived through the attack by a bull.

☐ b. only Mytum was a farmer.

☐ c. Stone had always had trouble with his bull, but Mytum had trusted his.

4. David Mytum said he would carry a stick until the bull was gone. What was the cause of his fear?

☐ a. The bull had attacked him once.

☐ b. The bull seemed sleepy.

☐ c. The bull kept knocking him down.

5. If you were a farmer, how could you use the information in the article to keep yourself safe?

☐ a. I would only raise quiet, good bulls.

☐ b. I would carry a stick when around bulls.

☐ c. I would trust bulls all the time.

Score 4 points for each correct answer.

_____ **Total Score:** Critical Thinking

Enter your score for each activity. Add the scores together. Record your total score on the graph on page 115.

_____ Finding the Main Idea

_____ Recalling Facts

_____ Making Inferences

_____ Using Words

_____ Author's Approach

_____ Summarizing and Paraphrasing

_____ Critical Thinking

_____ **Total Score**

Personal Response

I wonder why _____

_____

_____

Self-Assessment

One of the things I did well when reading this article was

_____

I believe I did this well because _____

_____

_____

A Child's Best Friend

Three-year-old Blake Weaver is shown here with his grandmother's dog Samantha.

Blake Weaver loved to play with his grandmother's dog. The dog's name was Samantha. She was a Rottweiler. Some people don't like Rottweilers. They say this kind of dog is too rough. They say Rottweilers don't make good pets. And they say these dogs should certainly never be turned loose near children. But the Weavers loved their dog. And Samantha loved them back. She even slept in Blake's bed. In 1996 this love saved the three-year-old boy's life.

2   It was January 24. Blake was in the backyard with Samantha. For some reason, Blake wandered off. Samantha went with him. A second family dog went too. At about 1:30 P.M., Blake's mother saw that Blake was not in the yard. Dawn Weaver called and called, but her little boy didn't answer. That worried her. She called the police. A search began. After a while, the second dog returned to the house. But there was no sign of Blake or Samantha.

3   The woods in this part of north Florida are thick. Even horses can't pass through some parts. To make things worse, it started to rain. It also grew colder. Florida nights can be cold in the winter. On this night, it would be close to freezing. Blake's mother remembered that Blake had been wearing just shorts, a T-shirt, and shoes. So the police tried to work fast. They used radios. They used search dogs. They used helicopters. They even used special tools that can spot warm bodies. Yet the hours passed, and still the police did not find Blake. "We found everything but him," said one officer.

4   No one knew it at the time, but Blake was in good hands—or at least good paws. Samantha never left the boy's side. The dog pushed Blake under some thick brush. That kept him dry. Samantha then pressed her body next to his. That kept him warm. Blake was scared, but with Samantha next to him, he did get some sleep.

5   All night the police searched. At one point, they closed the nearby roads. They wanted no noise from cars. They hoped they might hear the boy's crying, but they heard nothing.

6   When morning came, though, Samantha knew what to do. She got Blake to follow her out of the thick brush. She led him along a dirt path toward his home. About one mile from the Weavers' home, a woman named Debby Sundstrom saw them. Blake had no shoes or socks on. "He looked a little nervous," said Sundstrom. But after Sundstrom gave him a cookie, he felt better. "He was fine. He had a few scratches," said Sundstrom. Other than that, he was okay.

7   Dawn Weaver was happy to see her son. She wrapped Blake in a blanket and rushed him to a nearby hospital.

He had a cut on his face, he was red from the wind, and his feet hurt. But mostly he was just tired and happy to be safe.

8　Samantha had saved Blake's life. She had kept him from getting too scared. She had kept him dry. And she had kept him warm. The boy might have died. But with Samantha there, he was fine. "He wasn't even cold," said one officer.

9　Dawn Weaver was proud of Samantha. The dog had demonstrated how great Rottweilers can be. "I love them," Dawn said. "I think they are beautiful animals."

10　Samantha is not the only dog to save a child. Take the case of Francisco Queiros. In 2001 he was five years old. His family went on a trip to the mountains in Portugal. One day Francisco walked off. He soon got lost. Luckily, he had the family's three dogs with him.

11　Francisco's family had no idea where the boy was. They asked the police for help. Search teams began to check the woods. They had to hurry. A big storm was moving in. People searched all day and night. But they couldn't find Francisco. They began to fear the worst.

They worried they might soon be looking for a dead body instead of a live boy.

12　The next morning Francisco's uncle got lucky. He found the boy. The uncle couldn't believe it. Francisco was warm and dry. He wasn't hurt in any way. The three dogs had kept him safe all night. They had curled up on top of him. Their bodies had kept him from the wind and rain.

13　Dogs have even been known to save people they don't know. In Romania someone left a tiny baby girl under a picnic table. The baby was hidden in a bag. No human saw her. But a dog did. The dog stood watch over the girl. It began barking. At last, the dog got someone to notice. The little girl was rescued. It turned out that she was fine. But as one of her doctors said, "She was lucky."

14　There is an old saying in Portugal. "The greatest love is that of a mother. The second greatest love is that of a dog." The dogs in these stories saved three lives. They showed just how strong the love of a dog can be. 🎗

A | Finding the Main Idea

One statement below tells the main idea of the article. One statement is too general, or too broad. The other statement explains only part of the article; it is too narrow. Label the statements using the following key:

M—Main Idea   B—Too Broad   N—Too Narrow

_B_ 1. Over and over, dogs have proved themselves to be good friends to children in trouble.

_M_ 2. All over the world, animals can be counted on to help humans.

_N_ 3. After three-year-old Blake Weaver wandered into the woods, his grandmother's dog Samantha stayed with him until he was found.

Score 4 points for each correct answer.

_3_ **Total Score:** Finding the Main Idea

B | Recalling Facts

How well do you remember the facts in the article? Put an X in the box next to the answer that correctly completes each statement.

1. The brave and loving dog Samantha was a
   - ☐ a. beagle.
   - ☑ b. collie.
   - ☐ c. Rottweiler.

2. Samantha kept Blake Weaver dry by
   - ☐ a. lying next to him.
   - ☑ b. pushing him under thick brush.
   - ☐ c. barking loudly.

3. Francisco Queiros was kept safe in the woods all day and night by
   - ☐ a. a Rottweiler.
   - ☐ b. his uncle.
   - ☐ c. his family's three dogs.

4. A dog in Romania saved a baby girl's life when it
   - ☐ a. stood watch over her and barked until someone noticed
   - ☑ b. led her back to her family.
   - ☐ c. pressed its body close to her to keep her warm.

Score 4 points for each correct answer.

_4_ **Total Score:** Recalling Facts

C │ Making Inferences

When you draw a conclusion that is not directly stated in the text, you are making an inference. Put an X in the box next to the statement that is a correct inference.

1.

☐ a. The police probably rode horses through the woods when they looked for Blake Weaver.

☑ b. Winter days in Florida can be quite warm.

☐ c. Blake Weaver's mother never took her eyes off her son on the morning of January 24, 1996.

2.

☐ a. Rottweilers are the only dogs that love children.

☑ b. Francisco Queiros has always been afraid of his family's dogs.

☐ c. The Queiros family's dogs got wet and cold on the night they saved Francisco.

Score 4 points for each correct answer.

__2__ **Total Score:** Making Inferences

D │ Using Words

Put an X in the box next to the definition below that is closest in meaning to the underlined word.

1. Many people joined in the <u>search</u> for the lost child.

☐ a. the act of looking for something

☐ b. a surprise party

☐ c. a song that many people sing at the same time

2. It took weeks for the family to clear away <u>brush</u> so they could build a house.

☐ a. a sky filled with clouds

☐ b. water from a river or lake

☐ c. bushes growing close together

3. Logan felt <u>nervous</u> as he waited for the big test to begin.

☐ a. full of fear and worry

☑ b. happy and free of cares

☐ c. filled with anger

4. The <u>scratches</u> that the cat gave Trina turned an ugly red.

☐ a. hurt feelings

☐ b. cuts that are long but not deep

☐ c. the sounds a cat makes

5. Before we started the exercises, our teacher <u>demonstrated</u> how to do them.

☑ a. talked
☐ b. showed
☐ c. practiced

6. She was afraid that the <u>worst</u> would come true.

☐ a. something that is the oldest
☐ b. something that is the best
☐ c. something that is the most bad

Score 4 points for each correct answer.

<u>2</u> **Total Score:** Using Words

E | Author's Approach

Put an X in the box next to the correct answer.

1. The main purpose of the first paragraph is to

☐ a. tell how well Blake Weaver got along with his grandmother's dog.
☑ b. tell people that they shouldn't keep Rottweilers as pets.
☐ c. tell how the Weavers' dog saved Blake's life.

2. What purpose does the author give in paragraph 14 for writing the article?

☑ a. to tell people old sayings about dogs
☐ b. to tell stories that show how strong a dog's love can be
☐ c. to describe the people of Portugal

3. Choose the statement below that best explains how the author deals with the opposite point of view.

☐ a. The author says that Samantha, a Rottweiler, loved Blake Weaver.
☑ b. The author says that the Weaver family loved Samantha.
☐ c. The author says that some people believe Rottweilers are not good pets.

Score 4 points for each correct answer.

<u>3</u> **Total Score:** Author's Approach

F Summarizing and Paraphrasing

Put an X in the box next to the correct answer.

1. Which summary says all the important things about the article?

☐ a. Even though many people don't like Rottweilers, a Rottweiler named Samantha proved that these dogs can be loving.

☐ b. Once, a little girl was left in a bag under a picnic table in Romania. A dog that didn't even know her started barking. It barked until someone came. The little girl was fine.

☐ c. In Florida and in Portugal, dogs took care of little boys who had gotten lost in the woods. A dog also brought help to a little girl left in a bag in Romania.

2. Which sentence means the same thing as the following sentence? "Samantha never left the boy's side."

☐ a. Samantha stayed with the boy all the time.

☐ b. Samantha moved from side to side.

☐ c. Samantha brought the boy inside.

Score 4 points for each correct answer.

_____ **Total Score:** Summarizing and Paraphrasing

G Critical Thinking

Put an X in the box next to the correct answer.

1. Choose the statement below that states an opinion.

☐ a. Dawn Weaver loves Rottweilers.

☐ b. Francisco Queiros walked away from his parents on a trip to the mountains.

☐ c. Dogs are the best animals in the world.

2. From information in the article, you can predict that

☐ a. Dawn Weaver will not let her son sleep with Samantha again.

☐ b. the Queiros family will never take their dogs on trips again.

☐ c. the Weavers will always be glad that Samantha was with Blake that day.

3. Blake Weaver and Francisco Queiros are alike because

☐ a. both lived in north Florida and had pet Rottweilers.

☐ b. both were fine when they came back to their families.

☐ c. both were kept alive by three dogs.

4. Samantha pushed Blake under some thick brush. What was the effect of what the dog did?

☐ a. The police were able to find Blake.

☐ b. Blake stayed dry.

☐ c. Blake got very scared.

5. In which paragraph did you find the information or details to answer question 4?

☐ a. paragraph 4

☐ b. paragraph 6

☐ c. paragraph 7

Score 4 points for each correct answer.

_____ **Total Score:** Critical Thinking

Enter your score for each activity. Add the scores together. Record your total score on the graph on page 115.

_____ Finding the Main Idea

_____ Recalling Facts

_____ Making Inferences

_____ Using Words

_____ Author's Approach

_____ Summarizing and Paraphrasing

_____ Critical Thinking

_____ **Total Score**

Personal Response

I agree with the author because

_____

_____

Self-Assessment

When reading the article, I was having trouble with

_____

_____

Monkey Business in Hong Kong

The chase lasted two days. Then, at last, the police got their man. Or, to be more exact, they got their *monkey*.

2   The fun began on July 2, 2001. Someone spotted a monkey on a roof in Hong Kong. The police were called to take it away. But the monkey was too quick. Each time the police got close, it slipped away.

3   The chase went on for 10 hours. At dusk, the police gave up. It got too dark to see. But early the next day, the monkey was at it again. Someone noticed it sleeping on the roof of a small building. Before the police could grab it, it was gone. For the next five hours, the police tried to trap the monkey. They couldn't do it. Finally they lost sight of it near the harbor.

4   An hour later, someone saw it. This time it was sitting in a tree. But it was now on the other side of the harbor. How did it get over there? "We believe it took a ferry," said one officer. "A monkey can swim, but not very far."

5   No one saw the monkey on a ferry. But it might have found a good hiding place. In any case, the chase was on again. Police now held out bananas. They hoped the monkey would come to get the food. They tried oranges too. But the monkey was not interested.

6   By now, people had gathered to watch the chase. They cheered each time the monkey got away. The police thought of using a stun gun. With that special gun, they could keep the monkey from moving for a while. But there were too many people around. If they missed, they might hit a human. No one wanted to do that. So they kept trying to catch the monkey by hand.

7   Late in that second day, the monkey's luck turned. Two men cornered it. They could now fire a stun gun safely. One of the men did so. With that, the two-day chase ended. The monkey was not hurt. And the police later let it go. This one monkey did not bother people again. But Hong Kong's monkey problems were far from over.

8   At one time, Hong Kong had only a few monkeys. That changed in 1913. Hong Kong built a new lake to store drinking water. But poisonous plants grew near the water. No one wanted the plants to get into the drinking water. So monkeys were brought in to eat them. The plants did not hurt the monkeys. In fact, the monkeys loved them. With so much good food to eat, the number of monkeys grew.

Monkeys rest along the main road of Hong Kong's Monkey Mountain park. They are waiting to attack people who are carrying food.

9 Soon the hills around the lake were filled with monkeys. So was a nearby park. The park became known as Monkey Mountain. More than a thousand monkeys lived there. Many people came to watch them. People liked to see monkeys swing from tree to tree. They liked to watch them splash in the water. Some even liked to feed the monkeys.

10 The monkeys loved the human food. They learned to rip open bags of potato chips. They learned how to open cans of soda. The monkeys lost their fear of humans. They now *expected* to be fed. If a human did not bring them food, they got mad. If they got mad enough, they attacked.

11 "I've been attacked several times," said a man named Leung Mun-shing. "Once, a monkey jumped onto me and scratched my shoulder."

12 Some people took big sticks with them to the park. They used the sticks to keep monkeys away.

13 By 1999 it was clear that something had to be done. Hong Kong passed a new law. It said that anyone who fed the monkeys would be fined $10,000. People hoped that would make the monkeys start hunting for their own food again.

14 The plan worked—sort of. Monkeys did begin to hunt for food. But many did their hunting in the middle of Hong Kong! They left the mountain and walked to town. Some came into homes. They tried to take food from kitchens. Others went to food stores. They tried to grab people's bags as they left. Once, a band of 30 monkeys charged down the streets looking for food. People ran away in fear. The police had to set traps to catch them.

15 Hong Kong is still working to end its monkey problem. It has tried to keep monkeys from having babies. But the number of monkeys keeps growing. The police have tried to catch the monkeys that make trouble. They hope to send them to other parts of China or to zoos.

16 For now, the people of Hong Kong need to be careful. They need to follow three rules. First, they should not feed monkeys. Second, they should not get too close to monkeys. And third, they should not carry bags that look as though they might hold food. Then maybe people and monkeys can live near each other without trouble.

A | Finding the Main Idea

One statement below tells the main idea of the article. One statement is too general, or too broad. The other statement explains only part of the article; it is too narrow. Label the statements using the following key:

M—Main Idea   B—Too Broad   N—Too Narrow

_____ 1. For years, too many monkeys have bothered the people of Hong Kong, and now the city is trying to end the problem.

_____ 2. Sometimes trying to end one problem brings on a new and different problem.

_____ 3. In 1913 monkeys were brought into Hong Kong to eat poisonous plants near a lake filled with drinking water.

> Score 4 points for each correct answer.
>
> _____ **Total Score:** Finding the Main Idea

B | Recalling Facts

How well do you remember the facts in the article? Put an X in the box next to the answer that correctly completes each statement.

1. The police didn't want to use a stun gun against a monkey in Hong Kong because

☐ a. the monkey was too cute to hurt.
☐ b. they didn't want to hurt any humans.
☐ c. stun guns are too heavy to carry around.

2. The monkey probably reached the other side of the harbor by

☐ a. swinging from trees all the way there.
☐ b. taking a ferry.
☐ c. swimming there.

3. In 1999 Hong Kong passed a law that said

☐ a. anyone who fed a monkey would have to pay a fine.
☐ b. no one can kill a monkey.
☐ c. anyone who killed a monkey would get a prize.

4. To keep the number of monkeys from growing, Hong Kong has tried

☐ a. keeping monkeys in cages.
☐ b. feeding monkeys plenty of food to make them fat.
☐ c. stopping monkeys from having babies.

> Score 4 points for each correct answer.
>
> _____ **Total Score:** Recalling Facts

C Making Inferences

When you draw a conclusion that is not directly stated in the text, you are making an inference. Put an X in the box next to the statement that is a correct inference.

1.

☐ a. Most people now think that bringing monkeys to Hong Kong was a bad idea.

☐ b. Any plant that makes a human sick will also make an animal sick.

☐ c. Most people like having monkeys come into their homes.

2.

☐ a. Monkeys always act alone since they don't like being with other monkeys.

☐ b. It is very easy to get rid of animals that you don't want in a town.

☐ c. All the people of Hong Kong will have to work together to get rid of the problem with monkeys.

Score 4 points for each correct answer.

_____ **Total Score:** Making Inferences

D Using Words

Put an X in the box next to the definition below that is closest in meaning to the underlined word.

1. The street lights go on at dusk.

☐ a. time of day when the sun is overhead

☐ b. time of day when it starts to get light

☐ c. time of day when it starts to get dark

2. The captain hoped to get his ship into a nearby harbor before the storm hit.

☐ a. a body of water where boats can stay safely

☐ b. a large ship with many sails

☐ c. a club for people who own large boats

3. Driving cars onto the ferry is hard when the waves are high.

☐ a. a room or building in which new cars are sold

☐ b. an office building in the middle of a city

☐ c. a boat used to carry people and things across a body of water

4. Why do you always bother me with questions when I am on the phone?

☐ a. help

☐ b. make upset

☐ c. make happy

5. We took the baby to the doctor after she put a <u>poisonous</u> plant in her mouth.

☐ a. made of something that most people think tastes good

☐ b. having something that makes people or animals sick

☐ c. coming from another country

6. The little boy <u>expected</u> lots of gifts on his birthday.

☐ a. was afraid something might be coming

☐ b. threw away

☐ c. thought something should be coming

Score 4 points for each correct answer.

_____ **Total Score:** Using Words

E **Author's Approach**

Put an X in the box next to the correct answer.

1. The author uses the first sentence of the article to

☐ a. make the reader wonder who was being chased.

☐ b. describe Hong Kong's monkey problem.

☐ c. explain how monkeys came to Hong Kong.

2. Choose the statement below that best describes the author's opinion in paragraph 14.

☐ a. The new law ended the monkey problem.

☐ b. The new law was mean to the monkeys.

☐ c. The new law didn't work very well.

3. The author probably wrote this article in order to

☐ a. make readers afraid of monkeys.

☐ b. tell about an interesting problem.

☐ c. get the Hong Kong police to be nicer to monkeys.

Score 4 points for each correct answer.

_____ **Total Score:** Author's Approach

F | Summarizing and Paraphrasing

Put an X in the box next to the correct answer.

1. Which summary says all the important things about the article?

☐ a. In 1913 monkeys were brought into Hong Kong to eat poisonous plants. But now Hong Kong has too many monkeys. The city is trying to find a way to get rid of its problem.

☐ b. When the people of Hong Kong go to Monkey Mountain, they have to take sticks with them to keep the monkeys away from them and their food.

☐ c. Many monkeys live in the city of Hong Kong. People like to see them splash in the lake and swing from tree to tree.

2. Which sentence means the same thing as the following sentence? "No one wanted the plants to get into the drinking water."

☐ a. No one had enough drinking water.

☐ b. The plants were drinking too much water.

☐ c. People wanted to keep the plants out of the water they drank.

Score 4 points for each correct answer.

_____ **Total Score:** Summarizing and Paraphrasing

G | Critical Thinking

Put an X in the box next to the correct answer.

1. Choose the statement below that states a fact.

☐ a. People should treat monkeys better.

☐ b. Many monkeys were brought to Hong Kong in 1913.

☐ c. I like monkeys.

2. Monkeys and humans are different because

☐ a. the plants around the Hong Kong lake make only humans sick.

☐ b. only humans live in Hong Kong.

☐ c. only humans ride ferries from one side of the Hong Kong harbor to the other.

3. What was the effect of making it against the law to feed monkeys in Hong Kong?

☐ a. The monkeys came to town to look for food.

☐ b. The number of monkeys in Hong Kong went down quickly.

☐ c. The park around the lake became known as Monkey Mountain.

4. Which paragraphs provide information that supports your answer to question 3?

☐ a. paragraphs 15 and 16

☐ b. paragraphs 8, 9, and 10

☐ c. paragraphs 13 and 14

5. How are the monkeys of Hong Kong related to the topic of *Friend or Foe*?

☐ a. The monkeys started out as friends to humans but soon became foes.

☐ b. Humans are trying to be friends to the monkeys.

☐ c. Monkeys will always make trouble for humans.

Score 4 points for each correct answer.

_____ **Total Score:** Critical Thinking

Enter your score for each activity. Add the scores together. Record your total score on the graph on page 115.

_____ Finding the Main Idea

_____ Recalling Facts

_____ Making Inferences

_____ Using Words

_____ Author's Approach

_____ Summarizing and Paraphrasing

_____ Critical Thinking

_____ **Total Score**

Personal Response

Would you tell other students to read this article? Explain.

_____

Self-Assessment

One good question about this article that was not asked would be " _____?"

Compare and Contrast

Pick two stories in Unit One that tell about animals that have hurt people in some way.
Use information from the stories to fill in this chart.

Title	What is the worst thing that these animals have done or can do?	Why do these animals cause problems for people?	What can people do to stop the problems these animals cause?

Which of these animals scares you the most? Tell why you chose that animal. _____

_____

_____

UNIT TWO

Pigs to the Rescue

What do you think of when you hear the word *pet*? Some people think of a dog. Others think of a cat. Some might say a bird or a turtle. But how many would think of a pig?

2 That animal came to mind for Cathy Carder, of Winfield, West Virginia. Carder owned a potbellied pig named Iggy. She treated the pig like a member of her family. But in 2001, city leaders told her that Iggy had to go. They said it was against the law to keep a farm animal in the city.

3 Carder insisted that Iggy was a pet, not a farm animal. Indeed, potbellied pigs are a special kind of pig. They are much smaller than regular pigs. They are used to living in houses with people. Still, a judge told Carder she could not keep Iggy in Winfield.

4 Carder wouldn't leave her pig, so she sold her house and moved to Poca, 10 miles away. People there let Iggy live with her. It was a good thing they did.

Shown here is Carthy Carder with Iggy, her potbellied pig.

5 Less than a year later, Carder was taking a nap. Suddenly Iggy rushed into the room. The pig began making all sorts of strange noises. She grunted. She barked. At first, Carder didn't know what was wrong. Then she smelled smoke. The house was on fire! Thanks to Iggy, Carder and her two sons got out safely. The fire burned down their new home, but no one was hurt. Iggy was the hero of the day. "She is a wonderful animal," said Carder. "She saved our lives."

6 A potbellied pig also saved the lives of Pam and Rick Abma. The Abmas bought a baby pig when they got married in 1997. They named their pig Honeymoon. A year later, a fire broke out in the Abmas' laundry room. Honeymoon smelled the smoke. He raced to Pam and Rick's bedroom door. The pig threw himself against the door, screeching and grunting. At last Pam woke up. When she realized what was happening, she screamed to Rick, "The house is on fire!"

7 Rick ran to the bedroom door and opened it. The smoke was so thick he couldn't see much. Still, he managed to put out most of the fire. Firefighters soon came and put out the rest of the flames. Honeymoon's warning had come just in time. Without it, the house—and the Abmas—might have been lost.

8 Lulu is perhaps the most famous pig hero of all. She was the favorite pet of Jo Ann and Jack Altsman.

As a baby, LuLu weighed just four pounds. But by the time she was one year old, her weight was up to 150 pounds. The Altsmans also had a small dog named Bear. They had built a doggy door so Bear could go in and out whenever he wanted. At first, LuLu also used the door, but she soon grew too big for it. The Altsmans had to open the door for LuLu when she wanted to go out.

9   On August 4, 1998, Jack went fishing. Jo Ann stayed home with LuLu and Bear. Jo Ann, who was 57, had already had one heart attack. On this day, she had a second one. Right away, she knew it was a serious attack. As she fell to the floor, she screamed for help. "Somebody help me. Please help me."

10   That's when LuLu came to the rescue. "She looked at my head," said Jo Ann later. "She made sounds like she was crying."

11   LuLu headed for the tiny doggy door. Somehow she jammed her body through it, and then she raced for the main road. She ran into the middle of the road and plopped herself down. Drivers honked their horns. They slowed down, but they didn't stop. They just drove around her. Several times LuLu ran back to the house to check on Jo Ann. But each time she returned to the road and sat down again.

12   For a while, it looked as though she would never get anyone to stop and help. At last she rolled onto her back and stuck her four hoofs straight up—her "dead piggy trick." And it worked. A man stopped and followed LuLu back to the house. He shouted through the door that a pig was in trouble.

13   Jo Ann shouted back that she was in trouble too. She begged the man to call an ambulance.

14   With doctors' help, Jo Ann lived through her heart attack. But it was a close call. Just 15 more minutes and she probably would have died. LuLu had saved her life.

15   LuLu herself was hurt. She had cut her stomach while squeezing through the small doggy door. "She was bleeding. She was a mess," said Jo Ann. "How many humans would do that for you?" As a reward, Jo Ann gave LuLu her favorite food—a jelly doughnut.

16   LuLu became a national hero. A children's book was written about her, and the *New York Times* put her story on the front page. She appeared on TV shows around the world. She won the Trooper Award. It is given to animal heroes. LuLu was the first pig to win it. People called her the "Big Pig Who Could (And Did)."

17   A pig may not be your choice for a pet. But for the Carders, Abmas, and Altsmans, it was the perfect choice. And their pet pigs made the difference between life and death. ✾

A | Finding the Main Idea

One statement below tells the main idea of the article. One statement is too general, or too broad. The other statement explains only part of the article; it is too narrow. Label the statements using the following key:

M—Main Idea   B—Too Broad   N—Too Narrow

_____ 1. Not everyone likes the same kind of pet. Some unusual animals can make good pets.

_____ 2. The owners of three pigs learned that pet pigs can save their owners' lives.

_____ 3. Cathy Carder chose a pig to be her pet and was glad she did. The pig woke her up when her house was on fire and saved her life.

Score 4 points for each correct answer.

_____ **Total Score:** Finding the Main Idea

B | Recalling Facts

How well do you remember the facts in the article? Put an X in the box next to the answer that correctly completes each statement.

1. Cathy Carder had to move because

☐ a. city leaders said that her pig couldn't live in the city.

☐ b. her pig got too big to fit through the opening in her door.

☐ c. her pig bothered the neighbors.

2. The Abmas were glad they had their pig when he

☐ a. rushed into the room where Pam was napping and warned her that the house was on fire.

☐ b. threw himself against their bedroom door to warn them about a house fire.

☐ c. got a driver to stop and help Pam.

3. Usually, when LuLu the pig wanted to go outside,

☐ a. her owners had to open the door for her.

☐ b. she used the door the Altsmans had made for their dog.

☐ c. she climbed out the window in the kitchen.

4. A driver finally stopped when LuLu

☐ a. sat down in the road and refused to move.

☐ b. screeched and grunted and made other noises.

☐ c. did a trick that made her look like she was dead.

Score 4 points for each correct answer.

_____ **Total Score:** Recalling Facts

C | Making Inferences

When you draw a conclusion that is not directly stated in the text, you are making an inference. Put an X in the box next to the statement that is a correct inference.

1.

☐ a. LuLu had done the "dead piggy trick" at least once before she did it on the road.

☐ b. LuLu really didn't sense that something was wrong when her owner had the heart attack.

☐ c. The Altsmans didn't want anyone else to know about what their pig had done.

2.

☐ a. Pigs and dogs do not get along with each other and cannot live in the same house.

☐ b. Pigs enjoy looking at and smelling fires.

☐ c. Cathy Carder liked her pig better than she liked her first house.

Score 4 points for each correct answer.

_____ **Total Score:** Making Inferences

D | Using Words

Put an X in the box next to the definition below that is closest in meaning to the underlined word.

1. The men <u>grunted</u> loudly when they picked up the heavy table.

☐ a. made a deep sound in the throat

☐ b. shook hands with each other

☐ c. played a trick on one another

2. In the play, one woman started <u>screeching</u> loudly when she saw a mouse run under her bed.

☐ a. hitting with a stick

☐ b. hiding under the covers

☐ c. making a sharp, high sound

3. Because I was tired, I just <u>plopped</u> into the chair.

☐ a. banged

☐ b. fell heavily

☐ c. sat down carefully

4. After my uncle fell down, my aunt called an <u>ambulance</u> to take him to the hospital.

☐ a. someone trained to help sick people

☐ b. a car or truck that carries sick or hurt people

☐ c. a special phone used by hospitals

5. I will give a $100 <u>reward</u> to anyone who finds my cat.

☐ a. something given for a good act
☐ b. something done to punish for doing wrong
☐ c. a song or poem that tells a story

6. On <u>national</u> holidays, banks in the United States close.

☐ a. of a city or town
☐ b. of a neighborhood
☐ c. of a country

Score 4 points for each correct answer.

_____ **Total Score:** Using Words

E | Author's Approach

Put an X in the box next to the correct answer.

1. What is the author's purpose in writing this article?

☐ a. to get readers not to want dogs and cats for pets
☐ b. to tell readers why pigs make good pets
☐ c. to describe what happens during a heart attack

2. Choose the statement below that is the weakest argument for keeping a pet pig in the house.

☐ a. Pigs can help when there is trouble.
☐ b. Pigs can be loving animals.
☐ c. Pigs eat a lot and get really big.

3. Choose the statement below that best describes the author's opinion in paragraph 11.

☐ a. LuLu was too big for anyone to keep as a pet.
☐ b. LuLu showed that she cared about her owner.
☐ c. Drivers didn't even see LuLu in the middle of the road.

Score 4 points for each correct answer.

_____ **Total Score:** Author's Approach

F | Summarizing and Paraphrasing

Put an X in the box next to the correct answer.

1. Which summary says all the important things about the article?

- [ ] a. Most people don't think of pigs when they choose pets. Pigs, however, can be good pets for many reasons. So maybe more people should choose pigs for pets.
- [ ] b. LuLu the pig was too big to fit through a small doggy door safely. Even so, she squeezed through it several times to find someone to help her sick owner.
- [ ] c. Two pet pigs woke their owners when their houses were on fire. They saved their owners' lives. Another pig got help when her owner had a heart attack.

2. Which sentence means the same thing as the following sentence? "The pig threw himself against the door, screeching and grunting."

- [ ] a. The pig screeched and grunted as he threw himself against the door.
- [ ] b. The door made strange noises when the pig threw his body against it.
- [ ] c. When the pig was thrown against the door, he screeched and grunted.

Score 4 points for each correct answer.

_____ **Total Score:** Summarizing and Paraphrasing

G | Critical Thinking

Put an X in the box next to the correct answer.

1. Choose the statement below that states an opinion.

- [ ] a. The Altsmans' pig, LuLu, grew to weigh about 150 pounds.
- [ ] b. Jo Ann Altsman had her second heart attack on August 4, 1998.
- [ ] c. Potbellied pigs are the best kind of pet.

2. From information in the article, you can predict that

- [ ] a. firefighters will start carrying pigs on their trucks.
- [ ] b. most people will want pigs instead of dogs or cats from now on.
- [ ] c. all of these pig owners will treat their pets well for the rest of the pets' lives.

3. Iggy and Honeymoon are alike because both

- [ ] a. were bought just after their owners got married.
- [ ] b. warned people about a house fire.
- [ ] c. tried to put out a house fire.

4. A driver finally stopped and followed LuLu to Jo Ann Altsman's house. What was the cause of his stopping?

- [ ] a. LuLu was lying on her back in the road.
- [ ] b. LuLu was running back and forth from the road to the house.
- [ ] c. LuLu was grunting and screeching by the road.

5. Which paragraphs provide information that supports your answer to question 4?

☐ a. paragraphs 11 and 12

☐ b. paragraphs 8 and 16

☐ c. paragraphs 9 and 10

Score 4 points for each correct answer.

_____ **Total Score:** Critical Thinking

Enter your score for each activity. Add the scores together. Record your total score on the graph on page 115.

_____ Finding the Main Idea

_____ Recalling Facts

_____ Making Inferences

_____ Using Words

_____ Author's Approach

Summarizing and Paraphrasing

_____ Critical Thinking

_____ **Total Score**

Personal Response

How do you think Jo Ann Altsman felt when she heard the voice of the driver that LuLu had stopped?

_____

_____

Self-Assessment

While reading the article, _____ was the easiest for me.

No Safe Place

"The beast is dead," cried a man from the village.

2   The people of Chamiyari cheered. For the past month, they had lived in fear. A leopard had been prowling around the high mountains of India. This wild cat had killed five children. But now, in January of 2004, the leopard had been killed. People hoped that peace would now return to the village.

3   Sadly, things did not work out that way. Just one month later, another child was killed by a leopard. Perhaps the wrong cat had been killed earlier. Or perhaps there was more than one "man-eater" on the loose. In any case, five-year-old Sheetal did not stand a chance. She was near her home on February 11. Her mother was with her. Suddenly a leopard appeared. It moved with great speed. Sheetal was dead before her mother could do a thing.

4   Leopard attacks are a big problem in India—and not just in the mountains. In the 1970s, people feared that leopards were dying out. So India passed a law to save them. The law said no one could kill a leopard unless it attacked a human first. A leopard that attacked a human would be declared a "man-eater" and could be shot. The law worked. In fact, it may have worked too well. Since 1972 the number of wild cats has grown. Most leopards do not bother humans. They hunt deer, birds, monkeys, and other small creatures. But once in a great while, a man-eater comes along. And that means big trouble.

5   Leopards are not born man-eaters. But if a leopard gets hungry enough, it can turn into one. A leopard may get hungry when it grows old or gets hurt. It is no longer quick enough to catch a deer or a bird. It has to find something that is easier to hunt. That something is often a human.

6   Officials say that hunger led one leopard to become a man eater in 2003. This leopard stepped in a trap that someone had left in the forest. The leopard hurt its left paw in the trap. It also broke some teeth trying to bite its way out. In the end, it did escape. But it could no longer run fast. And its teeth could no longer cut through animal hides. It grew hungry and weak. At last, it began looking for humans to eat. It killed three children before officials shot it.

7   Such leopards are called *man*-eaters, but usually they attack children. Children are too weak to fight back.

The fierce-looking leopard pictured here is similar to the ones described in this story.

And children are easy to drag off. Leopards often attack a child when he or she is alone. But from time to time, they strike when an adult is around. In 1999 a woman named Balma Devi was walking home with her daughter. All at once, a leopard leaped out of the bushes. It went straight for Devi's little girl. For 10 minutes, Devi fought off the leopard. At last, the cat slipped away. Devi and her child were fortunate. They were not badly hurt. Later, forest officials shot and killed the leopard.

8 It's not just small villages that have this problem. Leopards strike even in large cities. Mumbai, formerly known as Bombay, is one of India's great cities. There is a huge nature park in the city. The park is filled with different kinds of plants and trees. It has lakes and caves. The park also has wild animals. As of 2003, about 40 leopards lived here.

9 Sometimes these leopards slip out of the park to look for food. Mostly they hunt small animals like dogs. But sometimes they go after humans. In 2003, four-year-old Anmol Bansal was near the park. Anmol lived in a nice neighborhood. It had its own playground. He was playing here when a leopard appeared. It grabbed Anmol and dragged him away.

10 Other children yelled and screamed at the cat. At last, the leopard let Anmol go. But it was too late. The boy died on his way to the hospital. It was the 23rd leopard attack of the year in Mumbai. Anmol was the 10th person of those who were attacked to die.

11 This deadly attack shocked people. "It is really weird that in a city like Bombay we have to live in fear of leopards," said one woman.

12 "I cannot believe that such a thing can happen," said Anmol's mother.

13 Parents near the park found themselves living in fear. Many had moved here because of the park's beauty. But now they didn't want to go near the park. They kept a close watch on their children. "I have to be with them all the time," said one mother. "When darkness falls, we take our children inside. No one knows when the leopards will appear."

14 Park officials scrambled to end the problem. They built a high wall around the park. They also began putting more small animals inside the park. They hoped the leopards would choose to hunt this natural food instead of humans. Only time will tell if these efforts will work. For now, though, people in India sometimes feel that no place is safe. The next leopard attack could happen to anyone, anywhere, at any time. ✤

A | Finding the Main Idea

One statement below tells the main idea of the article. One statement is too general, or too broad. The other statement explains only part of the article; it is too narrow. Label the statements using the following key:

M—Main Idea   B—Too Broad   N—Too Narrow

_____ 1. Animals such as leopards often cause problems for the humans who live near them.

_____ 2. In India, a law states that no one can kill a leopard unless it has already attacked a human.

_____ 3. The people of India live in fear of leopard attacks, especially now that a law to protect leopards has been passed.

Score 4 points for each correct answer.

_____ **Total Score:** Finding the Main Idea

B | Recalling Facts

How well do you remember the facts in the article? Put an X in the box next to the answer that correctly completes each statement.

1. Most leopards eat

☐ a. humans, especially children.
☐ b. the leaves, berries, and roots of plants.
☐ c. deer, birds, and other small animals.

2. A leopard will usually attack a person

☐ a. only when it has become weak and hungry.
☐ b. almost every time it sees a human walking alone.
☐ c. when that person has bothered it.

3. Mumbai is another name for the city called

☐ a. Bombay.
☐ b. Chamiyari.
☐ c. India.

4. To stop leopard attacks around the park in Mumbai, officials

☐ a. got rid of all the leopards in the park.
☐ b. stopped people from going into the park or building houses near the park.
☐ c. built a high wall around the park.

Score 4 points for each correct answer.

_____ **Total Score:** Recalling Facts

C | Making Inferences

When you draw a conclusion that is not directly stated in the text, you are making an inference. Put an X in the box next to the statement that is a correct inference.

1.

☐ a. Indian officials hope that leopards will die out soon because they are so dangerous to humans.

☐ b. Leopards attack humans only during the day.

☐ c. If not for the law that protects leopards, there would probably be fewer of these wild cats in India.

2.

☐ a. Hunger can make an animal do things it wouldn't do if it were well fed.

☐ b. Pets such as dogs are perfectly safe in the city of Mumbai.

☐ c. All leopards become man-eaters when they get too old to feed themselves by hunting other animals.

> Score 4 points for each correct answer.
>
> _____ **Total Score:** Making Inferences

D | Using Words

Put an X in the box next to the definition below that is closest in meaning to the underlined word.

1. The cat started slowly <u>prowling</u> around the attic, where it was sure a mouse was hiding.

☐ a. running at top speed toward a finish line

☐ b. roaming in a quiet, sly way

☐ c. napping, or going into a light sleep

2. After the terrible storm, city <u>officials</u> asked the state for money to build the town again.

☐ a. people who are visiting a place for a short time

☐ b. people who know a great deal about rocks and soil

☐ c. people in government who are in charge of something

3. We built a high fence in our backyard so that our dog could not <u>escape</u>.

☐ a. get away

☐ b. run

☐ c. sleep

4. The Johnston family felt <u>fortunate</u> that their house was still standing after the windstorm.

☐ a. lucky

☐ b. disappointed

☐ c. unhappy

5. I never eat food that I think looks <u>weird</u>.

☐ a. tasty
☐ b. fresh
☐ c. strange

6. Because of the <u>efforts</u> of everyone who worked for her and voted for her, the mayor kept her job.

☐ a. clothes worn by everyone who does a certain job; uniforms
☐ b. actions done to try to get something done
☐ c. events that are caused by other events

Score 4 points for each correct answer.

_____ **Total Score:** Using Words

E | Author's Approach

Put an X in the box next to the correct answer.

1. Choose the statement below that best describes the author's opinion in paragraph 14.

☐ a. Most people think that the officials' efforts will probably work.
☐ b. Most people think that the officials' efforts will probably not work.
☐ c. Most people are not sure if the officials' efforts will work.

2. The author probably wrote this article in order to

☐ a. get readers to visit India so they can see leopards.
☐ b. tell the reader about a problem with leopards in India.
☐ c. describe what happens when a leopard attacks a child.

3. The author tells this story mainly by

☐ a. describing what has happened to himself or herself.
☐ b. describing the experiences of several people.
☐ c. using his or her imagination.

Score 4 points for each correct answer.

_____ **Total Score:** Author's Approach

F | Summarizing and Paraphrasing

Put an X in the box next to the correct answer.

1. Which summary says all the important things about the article?

☐ a. Leopards that become old or weak sometimes have trouble feeding themselves. They may hunt humans, especially children, who are too weak to fight back.

☐ b. The number of leopards in India has grown since 1972, when a law to protect them was passed. Today, man-eating leopards are attacking people, especially children, and people all over India fear attacks.

☐ c. Parents of young children who live around the Mumbai nature park are afraid that leopards will attack their children. Officials are trying to keep leopards inside the park.

2. Which sentence means the same thing as the following sentence? "And its teeth could no longer cut through animal hides."

☐ a. Though the animals hid, their teeth were not very strong.

☐ b. Its teeth weren't strong enough to bite into hiding animals.

☐ c. Its teeth couldn't cut through animals' fur and skin.

Score 4 points for each correct answer.

_____ **Total Score:** Summarizing and Paraphrasing

G | Critical Thinking

Put an X in the box next to the correct answer.

1. Choose the statement below that states a fact.

☐ a. Officials are not trying very hard to solve the leopard problem.

☐ b. Man-eating leopards are a problem in both the mountain areas of India and in the city of Mumbai.

☐ c. India is the most dangerous place to live in the whole world.

2. Anmol Bansal and Sheetal were alike because

☐ a. both were killed by a leopard.

☐ b. both lived through a leopard attack.

☐ c. both lived near the big nature park in Mumbai.

3. What was the effect of one leopard's getting caught in a forest trap in 2003?

☐ a. The leopard killed the hunter who let him out of the trap.

☐ b. The leopard couldn't get out of the trap and died there.

☐ c. The leopard got weak and hungry and became a man-eater.

4. In which paragraph did you find the information or details to answer question 3?

☐ a. paragraph 3
☐ b. paragraph 5
☐ c. paragraph 6

5. Which lesson about life does this story teach?

☐ a. People and animals should never live near one another.

☐ b. People can't always control wild animals.

☐ c. People are happiest when they live in big cities.

Score 4 points for each correct answer.

_____ **Total Score:** Critical Thinking

Enter your score for each activity. Add the scores together. Record your total score on the graph on page 115.

_____ Finding the Main Idea

_____ Recalling Facts

_____ Making Inferences

_____ Using Words

_____ Author's Approach

_____ Summarizing and Paraphrasing

_____ Critical Thinking

_____ **Total Score**

Personal Response

I can't believe _____

_____

_____

Self-Assessment

From reading this article, I have learned _____

_____

Little Dogs and Big Bears

Pictured here are Don Mobley and his German shepherd, Shadow. Shadow saved Mobley from an attack by a huge grizzly bear.

Let's begin with a joke. How can you tell the difference between a black bear and a grizzly bear? First, get the bear really angry with you. Then find a tree and climb it. If the bear climbs up after you and eats you, it's a black bear. If the bear knocks the tree over and eats you, it's a grizzly bear.

2 Getting a bear mad at you, of course, is crazy. Bears are powerful animals. Their teeth and claws are deadly. But if anyone did want to get a bear angry, there is one foolproof way to do it. Just get between a mother bear and her cub. A mother bear will always attack if she thinks someone is about to hurt her baby.

3 Paul Guitard did not mean to scare a bear cub. He did it by accident. Guitard lived in Canada. He owned sled dogs. These dogs are not particularly big. A Siberian husky weighs only about 60 pounds. But they are strong, and they are tough. Working as a team, they can pull a very heavy load. They can go many miles without a rest.

4 One summer day in 1990, Guitard took his dogs out for a run through the woods. After about two miles, a bear suddenly appeared. "I looked over and saw two cubs on the path," Guitard said. By mistake, he had come between a mother and her cubs. Guitard knew all about bears. "Uh, oh," he thought to himself. "Now I'm in big trouble."

5 The bear attacked Guitard, biting him on the leg and arm. Guitard's dog team ran on without him. But after a hundred yards, the lead dog stopped. This dog had a bear's name—Grizzly. Grizzly looked back and saw what was happening. Although he was still tied to the other dogs, he turned around. He came racing toward the bear, dragging the other dogs with him. The bear was much bigger and heavier than Grizzly was, but the courageous dog kept on coming. He was ready to lay down his life to save his owner.

6 The bear let go of Guitard to confront the dog. Guitard ran away and began climbing the nearest tree. But that move did not make him safe. This bear was a black bear. It, too, could climb trees. Before Guitard got very high, the bear came after him again. It reached up, caught hold of Guitard's right leg, and bit it. "I was kicking her with my other foot, trying to make her let me go," said Guitard.

7 At that point, Grizzly moved in. He snapped and bit at the bear until it let go of Guitard's leg. Guitard then climbed higher. He was bleeding badly from his wounds and was in great pain. Meanwhile, Grizzly was trying to drive the bear away. He planted himself at the base of the tree and stood guard there. Each time the bear approached, Grizzly fought it off.

8 Grizzly fought the bear for almost seven hours.

At last, Guitard's friends came looking for him. He shouted to them, telling them to get a gun. When they returned with one, the bear charged them. They had no choice but to shoot it.

9   Guitard's wounds healed, and so did Grizzly's. The bear's claws had cut Grizzly's nose, but other than that he was in good shape. "I wouldn't be here if it weren't for that dog," said Guitard. "I'd be dead. That bear would have killed me."

10 Don Mobley ran into the same kind of trouble—except in his case, the bear was a grizzly. These bears are even bigger than black bears. Adult grizzlies don't climb trees. They are too big. But on the ground, they will fight fiercely. In fact, they are the fiercest of all bears.

11 In 2002 Mobley was gathering firewood near his home in Alaska. Luckily, he had his dog, Shadow, with him. Shadow was a German shepherd. Like Paul Guitard's dog, Shadow would do anything to protect his owner.

12 As Mobley picked up the wood, he saw a cub. The little bear was only 15 feet away. Knowing the mother would be close by, Mobley looked around. All at once, a huge grizzly bear jumped over a log and rushed straight at him. "She growled and came at me," said Mobley.

13 Mobley ran for a nearby river. "I didn't think I had any choice," he said. "I was going to get mauled."

14 Mobley knew he couldn't outrun the bear. But he hoped to get to the river before the bear got to him. Then perhaps the bear would give up. But the bear was gaining. It was within 10 feet of Mobley when suddenly, from out of nowhere, Shadow leaped at the bear. Barking wildly, the dog chased the bear into the woods. A few seconds later, Shadow came back. The dog was cut behind his ears, where the bear had either clawed or bitten him. But somehow Shadow had chased it away.

15 "He's a really tough dog," said Mobley. "The only thing that saved me was my dog."

16 Both Grizzly and Shadow had saved the lives of the ones they loved. In that sense, they were like the bears themselves. They were just protecting their families. ❦

A Finding the Main Idea

One statement below tells the main idea of the article. One statement is too general, or too broad. The other statement explains only part of the article; it is too narrow. Label the statements using the following key:

M—Main Idea   B—Too Broad   N—Too Narrow

_____ 1. Be careful in the woods because wild animals can be quite dangerous.

_____ 2. Don Mobley was out in the woods near his Alaska home when he ran into a bear cub and its angry mother.

_____ 3. When two men got between mother bears and their cubs, the men's dogs saved their lives.

Score 4 points for each correct answer.

_____ **Total Score:** Finding the Main Idea

B Recalling Facts

How well do you remember the facts in the article? Put an X in the box next to the answer that correctly completes each statement.

1. Paul Guitard tried to escape from the black bear by

☐ a. running into a cave.
☐ b. hiding behind his dogs.
☐ c. climbing a tree.

2. When Paul Guitard's dog Grizzly found out that Guitard was in trouble with a bear, it

☐ a. went to Guitard's friends for help.
☐ b. snapped and bit at the bear's leg.
☐ c. climbed the tree and guarded Guitard.

3. Don Mobley's dog was named

☐ a. Shadow.
☐ b. Blackie.
☐ c. Grizzly.

4. When Don Mobley's dog attacked the grizzly bear,

☐ a. the bear bit or clawed it behind its ears.
☐ b. the bear climbed a tree and roared loudly.
☐ c. Mobley's friends came to save him.

Score 4 points for each correct answer.

_____ **Total Score:** Recalling Facts

C | Making Inferences

When you draw a conclusion that is not directly stated in the text, you are making an inference. Put an X in the box next to the statement that is a correct inference.

1.

☐ a. Don Mobley was sure all along that his dog would be able to save his life.

☐ b. Both men are very grateful to their dogs.

☐ c. You can be sure that bears will run away from any animal that faces them with courage.

2.

☐ a. It is hard to make a bear give up when it is attacking someone.

☐ b. If you run away from a bear, it knows that you will not hurt its cub.

☐ c. A dog will never attack any animal that is bigger than itself.

Score 4 points for each correct answer.

_____ **Total Score:** Making Inferences

D | Using Words

Put an X in the box next to the definition below that is closest in meaning to the underlined word.

1. We had a <u>foolproof</u> plan. It couldn't go wrong.

☐ a. shaky

☐ b. unpopular

☐ c. sure

2. Even though he was wounded, the <u>courageous</u> soldier kept on fighting.

☐ a. brave

☐ b. silly

☐ c. lucky

3. After sneaking off with the cookies, the boy did not want to <u>confront</u> his mother.

☐ a. thank

☐ b. hurt

☐ c. face

4. All the other animals were afraid of the bear, the <u>fiercest</u> animal in the woods.

☐ a. most terrible

☐ b. most gentle

☐ c. smallest

5. The hunter was afraid he would be <u>mauled</u> by the lion when he got between it and its cub.

☐ a. thanked

☐ b. handled roughly

☐ c. forgotten

6. The winner will need to <u>outrun</u> every other person in the race.

☐ a. run faster than

☐ b. run toward

☐ c. run slower than

Score 4 points for each correct answer.

_____ **Total Score:** Using Words

E | **Author's Approach**

Put an X in the box next to the correct answer.

1. The main purpose of the first paragraph is to

☐ a. tell the reader about men who were attacked by bears.

☐ b. describe the dogs that saved the men's lives.

☐ c. compare black bears and grizzly bears.

2. From the statements below, choose the one that you believe the author would agree with.

☐ a. Most likely, the dogs in the article are the only two dogs that would be willing to fight for their owners.

☐ b. Some dogs are willing to give their lives to save their owners' lives.

☐ c. The only way to get away from an angry black bear is to climb a tree.

3. The author probably wrote this article in order to

☐ a. show that dogs are better pets than cats are.

☐ b. show that people don't need to be afraid of bears.

☐ c. show how brave dogs can be.

Score 4 points for each correct answer.

_____ **Total Score:** Author's Approach

F | Summarizing and Paraphrasing

Put an X in the box next to the correct answer.

1. Which summary says all the important things about the article?

☐ a. Paul Guitard came between a mother bear and her cub. The mother bear climbed up a tree after Guitard and might have killed him if his dog hadn't attacked the bear. After Don Mobley ran into a mother bear and her cub, his dog chased the bear into the woods and saved Mobley's life.

☐ b. Paul Guitard's dog Grizzly was a Siberian husky. When a bear attacked Guitard, Grizzly bravely kept the bear away from Guitard for seven hours. Guitard's friends had to shoot the bear.

☐ c. Don Mobley's dog probably saved his life. Mobley got between a mother bear and her cub. The mother bear chased Mobley for a while, but his dog surprised the bear and chased it away.

2. Which sentence means the same thing as the following sentence? "He did it by accident."

☐ a. He had planned on doing it.
☐ b. He didn't mean to do it.
☐ c. He is sorry that he did it.

Score 4 points for each correct answer.

_____ **Total Score:** Summarizing and Paraphrasing

G | Critical Thinking

Put an X in the box next to the correct answer.

1. Choose the statement below that states a fact.

☐ a. A Siberian husky weighs about 60 pounds.
☐ b. Siberian huskies are braver than German shepherds.
☐ c. Dogs are braver than bears.

2. Black bears and grizzly bears are different because

☐ a. only black bears try to protect their cubs.
☐ b. only black bears can climb trees.
☐ c. only grizzly bears live in wooded areas.

3. What was the effect of the bear's charging Paul Guitard's friends?

☐ a. Guitard's dog began barking at the bear and guarding Guitard.
☐ b. The friends ran away into the woods.
☐ c. The friends had to shoot the bear.

4. In which paragraph did you find the information or details to answer question 3?

☐ a. paragraph 4
☐ b. paragraph 9
☐ c. paragraph 8

5. Which lesson about life does this story teach?

☐ a. Dogs can be very loyal to their owners, even in dangerous times.

☐ b. There is no way of knowing what makes any animal angry.

☐ c. If you are small, you have no power over something or someone bigger than you.

Score 4 points for each correct answer.

_____ **Total Score:** Critical Thinking

Enter your score for each activity. Add the scores together. Record your total score on the graph on page 115.

_____ Finding the Main Idea

_____ Recalling Facts

_____ Making Inferences

_____ Using Words

_____ Author's Approach

_____ Summarizing and Paraphrasing

_____ Critical Thinking

_____ **Total Score**

Personal Response

A question I would like Paul Guitard to answer is

"_____ ?"

Self-Assessment

Before reading this article, I already knew

_____

_____

Danger in the Sky

As soon as the jet took off from Cincinnati, the pilot sensed trouble. One of the plane's engines was losing power. Then a second engine stopped dead. There was no way the jet could go on. And so, on February 22, 1999, the pilot turned around and landed fast. No one on the plane was hurt, but it was a close call.

2   A year and a half later, a jet took off from Los Angeles. There were 449 passengers on board. People on the ground heard a loud noise. They saw flames shoot from the plane. Parts of one engine fell to the ground. The pilot knew the jet might soon catch on fire, so he dumped most of the plane's fuel over the ocean. Then he made a quick landing. Once again, no one was hurt.

3   In Philadelphia that same month, one jet never got off the ground. As the plane was about to take off, one of its engines failed. By then the plane was going very fast. The pilot knew he was in big trouble. He slammed on the brakes. The plane stopped so fast that nine tires blew out.

4   What caused these problems? In all three cases, the answer was the same: birds. In the first case, the jet hit a flock of about 400 birds. In the next case, the jet engine sucked in a large bird. In the third case, 30 geese hit the plane.

5   Large jets are not the only ones in danger. Birds hit small planes and helicopters too. In 2001 a helicopter was on its way to a Missouri hospital. A heart patient was on board. Suddenly, a duck smashed through the pilot's window. The flying glass hurt the pilot. He managed to land safely, but the heart patient got quite a shock. The dead duck landed right in the patient's lap.

6   Most of the time, birds don't cause too much harm to planes. But they can ruin engines. They can harm a plane's body. They can even kill people. It doesn't happen often, but it does happen.

7   One of the worst accidents with birds and planes occurred in Anchorage, Alaska. The date was September 22, 1995. The jet was a U.S. Air Force plane. It had four jet engines. The $200 million plane had a fine safety record. But on this day, trouble began right away. As the plane gained speed to take off, something went wrong. People on the ground saw the trouble begin.

An airport worker holds up a falcon at Malaga airport in Spain. A team of 12 falcons are used at this airport to hunt and kill small birds that sometimes get sucked into jet engines.

Flames shot out of one engine. A burst of sparks followed. Still, the plane lifted off.

8   The plane banked left, but then it lost power and dove straight down. The jet crashed into the woods just beyond the airport. A giant ball of fire rose into the sky. All 24 people on board died.

9   Experts later found that the jet had flown into a flock of geese. Five of these birds had been sucked into the two left engines. It was simply a matter of bad luck. If the jet had taken off a few seconds earlier, it would have missed the birds. If it had taken off a few seconds later, it would have missed the birds.

10   The problem of birds and planes is a good example of "friend or foe?" Many people love birds. They want to protect them. But birds tend to live near low, wet land—and this is just the kind of land used for airports. Airports are built on low, wet land because most good, dry land has already been used for homes and businesses.

11   Birds find plenty of feeding grounds near airports. There are large pieces of land set aside for wildlife. Golf courses, parks, and lawns offer sweet grass that birds love. So in many cities, the number of birds has grown.

Take Anchorage as an example. Once there were just a few hundred geese in this city. But by 1996, the number was close to 5,000. One pilot admitted that his airplane hit birds "quite a bit." Even Alaskans in cars had trouble. Sometimes there were so many geese in the road that all cars had to stop.

12   The deaths of the 24 people on the Air Force jet forced Alaska to act. There were just too many birds. So Alaskans took several steps. They captured young birds and moved them to distant spots. They got rid of the sweet grass in parks. They put in plants that geese do not like to eat. And they set up horns around the airport. These horns could be blasted to scare away any birds that got too close. If that didn't work, airport workers shot at the birds.

13   By 2002 the number of geese in Anchorage was down to 1,500. Alaskans had made the air safer for planes as well as birds. But in other places, the danger remains high. Experts say that each year birds and planes hit each other more than 2,000 times. That doesn't make the "friendly skies" sound so friendly after all. ✒

A | Finding the Main Idea

One statement below tells the main idea of the article. One statement is too general, or too broad. The other statement explains only part of the article; it is too narrow. Label the statements using the following key:

M—Main Idea   B—Too Broad   N—Too Narrow

_____ 1. In 1995 a plane taking off in Anchorage, Alaska, sucked five birds into its engines and crashed.

_____ 2. Thousand of times each year, birds run into planes, sometimes causing harm to planes and lost lives.

_____ 3. Even though it seems as if a small bird could do no harm, birds do sometimes cause trouble.

Score 4 points for each correct answer.

_____ **Total Score:** Finding the Main Idea

B | Recalling Facts

How well do you remember the facts in the article? Put an X in the box next to the answer that correctly completes each statement.

1. When a jet flying from Cincinnati ran into a flock of birds, its pilot

☐ a. crashed the plane into woods.
☐ b. dumped the plane's fuel into the ocean.
☐ c. turned the plane around and landed it.

2. A duck ran into a

☐ a. helicopter on its way to a hospital.
☐ b. jet on its way to Los Angeles.
☐ c. helicopter on its way to Anchorage, Alaska.

3. Airports are often built on

☐ a. hilly land.
☐ b. wet land.
☐ c. dry land.

4. One way that the Anchorage airport solved its bird problem was by

☐ a. putting in plants that the geese don't like to eat.
☐ b. moving the airport to a drier piece of land.
☐ c. putting an electric fence around the airport.

Score 4 points for each correct answer.

_____ **Total Score:** Recalling Facts

C Making Inferences

When you draw a conclusion that is not directly stated in the text, you are making an inference. Put an X in the box next to the statement that is a correct inference.

1.

☐ a. Many birds are frightened by loud noises.

☐ b. It is not possible for something as small and light as a duck to break the window of a helicopter.

☐ c. When it comes to running into birds in the air, people are safer in a big plane than in a helicopter.

2.

☐ a. Birds in Alaska give people more trouble than birds anywhere else do.

☐ b. Good pilots can easily make sure they don't hit birds in the air.

☐ c. To work right, a jet engine needs to pull air into it.

Score 4 points for each correct answer.

_____ **Total Score:** Making Inferences

D Using Words

Put an X in the box next to the definition below that is closest in meaning to the underlined word.

1. All the nurses agreed that my grandfather was the most difficult <u>patient</u> in the west wing of the hospital.

☐ a. a problem

☐ b. a sick person

☐ c. a helper

2. Lucy jumped when the phone <u>suddenly</u> rang.

☐ a. in an angry way

☐ b. slowly and carefully

☐ c. without warning

3. <u>Experts</u> who have studied the problem agree that Americans eat too much junk food.

☐ a. people who know nothing about a certain thing

☐ b. people who know a lot about a certain thing

☐ c. people who are not interested in much

4. The boy <u>admitted</u> that he had broken the window and said that he would fix it.

☐ a. said it was so

☐ b. said that it could not be so

☐ c. said one was not sure

5. On summer nights, the children <u>captured</u> fireflies and then set them free again.

☐ a. killed
☐ b. spied
☐ c. caught

6. That city is so <u>distant</u> that it will take us three days to drive there.

☐ a. far away
☐ b. nearby
☐ c. busy

Score 4 points for each correct answer.

_____ **Total Score:** Using Words

E | Author's Approach

Put an X in the box next to the correct answer.

1. What is the author's purpose in writing this article?

☐ a. to get the reader to stop feeding birds
☐ b. to tell the reader about how the people in Anchorage, Alaska, got rid of geese
☐ c. to describe what happens when birds run into planes and helicopters

2. Choose the statement below that best explains how the author deals with the opposite point of view.

☐ a. The author tells about all the trouble that birds cause.
☐ b. The author explains that people love birds even if they cause trouble.
☐ c. The author tells how Anchorage, Alaska, got rid of many birds.

3. The author tells this story mainly by

☐ a. telling different stories about the same topic.
☐ b. comparing different topics.
☐ c. using his or her imagination.

Score 4 points for each correct answer.

_____ **Total Score:** Author's Approach

F Summarizing and Paraphrasing

Put an X in the box next to the correct answer.

1. Which summary says all the important things about the article?

☐ a. There are many examples of accidents in which birds that hit planes have caused damage and death. One airport in Anchorage, Alaska, has taken steps to solve the problem.

☐ b. Birds like to eat the grass in the open spaces around airports. In the last several years, the number of birds around airports has grown.

☐ c. To get rid of birds near their airport, Alaskans have begun to take young birds to distant areas, frighten birds with loud horns, take away their sweet grass, and even shoot at them.

2. Which sentence means the same thing as the following sentence? "But birds tend to live near low, wet land."

☐ a. Birds usually choose not to live near low, wet land.

☐ b. Birds should not be allowed to live near low, wet areas.

☐ c. Birds are likely to live near low, wet land.

Score 4 points for each correct answer.

_____ **Total Score:** Summarizing and Paraphrasing

G Critical Thinking

Put an X in the box next to the correct answer.

1. Choose the statement below that states an opinion.

☐ a. In 1996 Anchorage, Alaska, was home to about 5,000 geese.

☐ b. Airport officials should be allowed to poison birds near the airport.

☐ c. When a duck hit a helicopter in 2001, the duck landed in a heart patient's lap.

2. The problem the jet in Los Angeles had and the problem that the jet in Anchorage had are alike because in both cases

☐ a. the jet went through flocks of birds so thick that the pilot could not see.

☐ b. birds went through the jet's windows.

☐ c. birds were sucked into the jet engines.

3. What was the cause of the problem that the jet in Cincinnati had in 1999?

☐ a. The jet hit a flock of about 400 birds.

☐ b. The jet engine sucked in a large bird.

☐ c. A flock of about 30 geese hit the jet.

4. Which paragraphs provide information that supports your answer to question 3?

☐ a. paragraphs 1, 2, and 3

☐ b. paragraphs 1 and 4

☐ c. paragraphs 7 and 9

5. If you were in charge of building an airport, how could you use the information in the article to find a good place to build it?

☐ a. I would build the airport in a place with only a few birds.

☐ b. I would put the airport in a place that had many birds.

☐ c. I would build the airport near low, wet land.

Score 4 points for each correct answer.

_____ **Total Score:** Critical Thinking

Enter your score for each activity. Add the scores together. Record your total score on the graph on page 115.

_____ Finding the Main Idea

_____ Recalling Facts

_____ Making Inferences

_____ Using Words

_____ Author's Approach

_____ Summarizing and Paraphrasing

_____ Critical Thinking

_____ **Total Score**

Personal Response

If you could ask the author of the article one question, what would it be? _____

_____

_____

Self-Assessment

While reading the article, _____

_____ was the easiest for me.

Compare and Contrast

Pick two stories in Unit Two that taught you animal facts that you hadn't known before.
Use information from the stories to fill in this chart.

Title	What is one animal fact that you learned from this story?	What did an animal in this story do that surprised you?	How does an animal in this story help or hurt people?

From the stories choose an animal that you would like to learn more about. Tell why. _____

_____

_____

UNIT THREE

Small but Deadly

This photo is a close-up shot of a mosquito on human skin.

No one likes mosquitoes. And that makes sense. Nothing is more annoying than a mosquito buzzing around your head. And a mosquito in your ear can drive you mad. But if you think mosquitoes are just annoying, think again. The truth is they can be deadly. Mosquitoes have killed more people than all the wars in history.

2 Mosquitoes kill by spreading diseases. When a mosquito bites you, it may leave you with just an itchy red mark. Or it might leave you with a deadly disease. Mosquitoes don't get sick from the diseases they carry. But humans do.

3 One disease that mosquitoes carry is malaria. It kills about a million people a year. Malaria begins with chills and a fever. Then comes a crushing headache. Malaria can be treated. But if it isn't treated, it can kill you.

4 Then there's dengue fever. It, too, gives you fever and chills. It also makes your joints and muscles very sore. In fact, the pain is so great it feels as if your bones are breaking. That's why dengue is also called breakbone fever.

5 Elephantiasis is also spread by mosquitoes. This disease makes your legs puff up until they seem like they are the size of an elephant's. This change happens because tiny worms start growing inside your body. They get in your blood and make parts of your body swell.

6 Another disease carried by mosquitoes, the West Nile virus, starts off by making you sleepy. Your skin breaks out, and you get a pain in your stomach. Then your brain starts to swell. While most people recover from this disease, some die.

7 These diseases strike most often in hot, wet parts of the world. They have been around in Asia and Africa for a long time. But lately they have been spreading. They have even begun to show up in North America.

8 In 2002 an Illinois woman named Liz Larmin was getting her children ready for school. Suddenly she got a blinding headache and felt sick to her stomach. Her husband thought it was just a mild illness, but Larmin had a feeling it was something much worse. "I felt I had West Nile," she said. "I just knew in my bones."

9 She was right. By the next day, Larmin had developed a high fever and could barely walk. At the hospital, her doctors told her she had the West Nile virus. The disease didn't kill her. But it took a long time for her to get her strength back.

10 "I never liked bugs before," said Larmin. "Now I totally hate them."

11 Another woman, Joan Buchanan, had an even tougher time with the disease. She also got the West Nile virus in 2002. Buchanan was recovering from cancer at the time, so her body was already weakened.

When she got West Nile, she fell into a deep sleep called a *coma,* and she didn't wake up for a week. Even after she woke up, Buchanan needed a machine to help her breathe. She couldn't talk or move. The best she could do was smile.

12   It took months for Buchanan to recover. There's not much that can be done for people who get West Nile. A victim just has to live through it and hope to get better. And getting better can be a slow process.

13   Buchanan's husband said that before the cancer treatments, mosquitoes had always gone after him, not her. The treatments seemed to change that. "It seemed to make her sweet to mosquitoes," he said. Indeed, experts say that mosquitoes do like some people more than others. Each person has a slightly different smell. So mosquitoes can pick and choose. Some people are rarely bitten. Others get bitten all the time.

14   Not all types of mosquitoes bite people. Male mosquitoes never bite. They can't. Their mouths are not built for biting. They feed only on flowers and plants. A female, on the other hand, needs blood to make eggs. It will bite humans or animals. If a female mosquito isn't swatted away, it will drink until its belly is full.

15   What can you do to lower the chances of being bitten? First, use bug spray. Wear long pants and shirts with long sleeves. Also, mosquitoes are less likely to bite someone wearing white clothing. Be extra careful at dawn and in the early evening, since that's when most mosquitoes like to eat. Mosquitoes can get to you indoors too. So be sure there are no holes in your screen doors and windows.

16   Another way to cut down on mosquito bites is to lower the number of mosquitoes. Mosquitoes lay eggs in standing water. They love old tires and rain gutters. They love empty cans and barrels too. Even dishes left outside will do. Getting rid of these things will make it harder for mosquitoes to lay their eggs.

17   Still, we are never going to get rid of all mosquitoes. There are just too many of them. There are about 2,700 different kinds. And they live all over the globe. They're found in valleys and on mountains. Many live where it is warm. But some live in the Arctic Circle. We may wish mosquitoes would just go away. But these tiny critters will probably always be around to bug us. 🎗

A | Finding the Main Idea

One statement below tells the main idea of the article. One statement is too general, or too broad. The other statement explains only part of the article; it is too narrow. Label the statements using the following key:

M—Main Idea   **B—Too Broad**   **N—Too Narrow**

_____ 1. Joan Buchanan was recovering from cancer when she got the deadly West Nile virus, which almost killed her.

_____ 2. Some insects are not only annoying; they can also be dangerous.

_____ 3. Mosquitoes can spread many kinds of serious, even deadly, diseases.

Score 4 points for each correct answer.

_____ **Total Score:** Finding the Main Idea

B | Recalling Facts

How well do you remember the facts in the article? Put an X in the box next to the answer that correctly completes each statement.

1. A mosquito spreads disease by

☐ a. landing on its victims and letting its legs touch them.

☐ b. biting its victims.

☐ c. breathing on its victims.

2. Every year, malaria kills about

☐ a. one million people.

☐ b. 10,000 people.

☐ c. 50 million people

3. Liz Larmin was sure she had the West Nile virus when she

☐ a. developed a bad rash.

☐ b. got a terrible headache.

☐ c. got dizzy and fell down.

4. A female mosquito bites people and animals because it

☐ a. likes the taste of blood.

☐ b. wants to find a place for its eggs to hatch.

☐ c. needs blood to make its eggs.

Score 4 points for each correct answer.

_____ **Total Score:** Recalling Facts

C Making Inferences

When you draw a conclusion that is not directly stated in the text, you are making an inference. Put an X in the box next to the statement that is a correct inference.

1.

☐ a. Only people in North America need to worry about getting a disease from a mosquito.

☐ b. If you want to get away from mosquitoes, you just need to go to the Arctic Circle.

☐ c. It is hard for a human body to fight two diseases at the same time.

2.

☐ a. If you are never bitten by mosquitoes, you probably will not get the West Nile virus.

☐ b. Mosquitoes can live only in places where it is very hot and wet all the time.

☐ c. Mosquitoes have no sense of smell.

Score 4 points for each correct answer.

_____ **Total Score:** Making Inferences

D Using Words

Put an X in the box next to the definition below that is closest in meaning to the underlined word.

1. If you catch a harmful <u>virus</u>, you might not feel well for a long time.

☐ a. an insect similar to the honeybee

☐ b. a scarf or warm hat from Asia

☐ c. a very small thing that causes illness

2. The clerk seemed <u>totally</u> surprised when everyone shouted "happy birthday!"

☐ a. partly

☐ b. completely

☐ c. helpfully

3. The <u>process</u> of painting the house took longer than we thought it would take.

☐ a. a picture of several natural objects

☐ b. a number of steps that together get a job done

☐ c. a mustard yellow color

4. Sometimes the <u>treatments</u> for an illness hurt more than the illness itself.

☐ a. actions done to entertain people

☐ b. actions done to make someone ill

☐ c. actions done to cure an illness

5. Mother <u>swatted</u> flies away from the cake on the picnic table.

☐ a. slapped
☐ b. sang
☐ c. welcomed

6. Our picnic was spoiled by ants, flies, and other tiny <u>critters</u>.

☐ a. animals
☐ b. beings from outer space
☐ c. high winds

Score 4 points for each correct answer.

_____ **Total Score:** Using Words

E | Author's Approach

Put an X in the box next to the correct answer.

1. The main purpose of the first paragraph is to

☐ a. describe the diseases mosquitoes spread.
☐ b. tell how dangerous mosquitoes can be.
☐ c. tell exactly how mosquitoes spread diseases.

2. What is the author's purpose in writing this article?

☐ a. to get the reader to try to wipe out mosquitoes
☐ b. to tell the reader about Joan Buchanan's illness
☐ c. to describe what happens sometimes when mosquitoes bite people

3. Choose the statement below that best describes the author's opinion in paragraph 17.

☐ a. There are about 2,700 kinds of mosquitoes.
☐ b. Mosquitoes are dangerous insects.
☐ c. Mosquitoes are here to stay.

Score 4 points for each correct answer.

_____ **Total Score:** Author's Approach

F Summarizing and Paraphrasing

Put an X in the box next to the correct answer.

1. Which summary says all the important things about the article?

☐ a. Mosquitoes spread many illnesses, including malaria, breakbone fever, elephantiasis, and the West Nile disease. When you get the West Nile virus, you feel sleepy at first. Then you get a skin rash and stomach pain, and your brain starts to swell.

☐ b. Mosquitoes have spread diseases in the blood of their victims. Recently, mosquitoes have spread the West Nile virus in North America and made many people sick, including two women who almost died. There are ways of lowering the chances of getting bitten by mosquitoes that carry diseases.

☐ c. Liz Larmin was getting her children ready for school when she felt the West Nile virus coming on. She got to the hospital in time to be saved. Joan Buchanan went into a coma when she got the West Nile virus.

2. Which sentence means the same thing as the following sentence? "Malaria can be treated."

☐ a. Doctors have ways to cure malaria.
☐ b. We can treat people with malaria kindly.
☐ c. Having malaria is a real treat.

G Critical Thinking

Put an X in the box next to the correct answer.

1. Choose the statement below that states a fact.

☐ a. Everyone hates mosquitoes.
☐ b. There are about 2,700 kinds of mosquitoes.
☐ c. Experts should find ways to get rid of all dangerous mosquitoes.

2. From information in the article, you can predict that

☐ a. people will soon stop being afraid of viruses.
☐ b. no one else will ever die of a virus again.
☐ c. doctors will look for ways to stop viruses from killing people.

3. Male and female mosquitoes are different because

☐ a. only females bite.
☐ b. only females feed on flowers and plants.
☐ c. only males spread disease.

4. In which paragraph did you find the information or details to answer question 3?

☐ a. paragraph 13
☐ b. paragraph 14
☐ c. paragraph 16

Score 4 points for each correct answer.

_____ **Total Score:** Summarizing and Paraphrasing

5. How is the mosquito an example of an animal that is a friend or a foe to humans?

☐ a. The mosquito is a foe to humans because it spreads diseases and annoys people.

☐ b. The mosquito is a friend to humans because it lives all over the globe.

☐ c. It is hard to say whether the mosquito is a friend or a foe to humans.

Score 4 points for each correct answer.

_____ **Total Score:** Critical Thinking

Enter your score for each activity. Add the scores together. Record your total score on the graph on page 115.

_____ Finding the Main Idea

_____ Recalling Facts

_____ Making Inferences

_____ Using Words

_____ Author's Approach

_____ Summarizing and Paraphrasing

_____ Critical Thinking

_____ **Total Score**

Personal Response

Describe a time when you were annoyed by mosquitoes.

_____

_____

Self-Assessment

A word or phrase in the article that I do not understand is

_____

_____

The Kangaroo Problem

Sylvia Aldren just wanted to pick some flowers. On March 16, 2004, Aldren walked out to her garden in Brisbane, Australia. She began to gather roses. Then she saw a large kangaroo standing nearby. There are millions of kangaroos in Australia. So Aldren was not too surprised to see one, although she lived near a big city. What did surprise her, though, was the way this kangaroo stared at her.

2 "The look in the kangaroo's eye made me feel that I knew I was in trouble," she said. "I thought this is it; he's going to kill me."

3 The next thing she knew, the kangaroo was jumping at her. It knocked her down, and then it dug its claws into her back.

4 "I tried to get up four or five times," she later said, "but he kept kicking me over. He also bit my hand."

5 Luckily, neighbors came to her rescue. But by then, Aldren was bleeding badly. She was rushed to the

---

The kangaroos shown here are similar to the ones described in the story.

nearest hospital with scratches and bite marks all over her body.

6 It was not the first time a kangaroo had attacked a human. In 2003 a kangaroo followed Doug Lawton into his home in Queensland. It attacked Doug and his wife, Pauline. Doug grabbed a broom and tried to push the kangaroo away, but it knocked him down. It punched Doug with its paws. Then it turned and pounced on Pauline. Luckily, the couple managed to scare it off before it hurt them too badly.

7 John Crouch could not scare off the kangaroo that attacked him. He was in the yard of a home in Queensland when it jumped on him. First the kangaroo scratched and bit him. Next it attacked his wife, Helen. The creature kicked her in the stomach and clawed at her face, back, and legs.

8 Desperate to stop the attack, John picked up an axe. He swung it at the kangaroo until the animal was dead.

9 "It was kill or be killed," John later said. "I'm absolutely sure it would have killed us if it could."

10 Why are kangaroos attacking people? And what should be done about it? In Australia, these questions are on everyone's lips. But so far, people can't agree on any answers.

11 Many people love kangaroos. They love to see a baby kangaroo peek its head out from its mother's pouch.

And people love to watch kangaroos move. These creatures can hop at speeds of up to 50 miles per hour. They can cover up to 30 feet in a single bounce.

12 Kangaroos have been in Australia for 15 million years. Until recently, they weren't a problem. But in the 1900s, humans began to kill too many of them. Their numbers dropped. Australia passed laws to end the killing. The laws helped bring the numbers back up. Kangaroos also got help from farmers. Farmers ran water pipes across the land. These pipes were meant to keep crops from dying during droughts. But they kept kangaroos from dying too. The pipes gave the animals sufficient water to drink and grass to eat.

13 As a result, the number of kangaroos kept rising. Today there are 60 million of them. Far more kangaroos live in Australia than ever before. Huge kangaroo packs roam the land. Some attack humans in hopes of getting food. Some seem to attack for no reason at all.

14 Those who are afraid of being attacked would like to see the kangaroo population brought down. So would farmers. Farmers complain that kangaroos eat their crops. Paul Remond says that kangaroos eat up to half his wheat crop every year. Kangaroos also eat grass that is meant for his sheep.

15 The government knows there is a problem. It has agreed to let hunters and farmers kill kangaroos. Up to 5.2 million can be killed each year. Farmers say this number is too low. But wildlife experts say it is too high. These experts point out that there are 47 kinds of kangaroos. A few do have large populations. But others are quite rare. Experts fear that the rare ones will be killed by mistake. They also worry that the animals won't be killed in a humane way.

16 Some people say that kangaroos should not be killed at all. They believe that kangaroos are our friends. Leonard Richards would probably agree with that point of view. In the early 1990s, Richards found a baby kangaroo. Its mother had been killed by a car. Richards brought the baby home. He fed it with a bottle and named it Lulu. Later he released Lulu into the wild. But she stayed nearby. She often followed Richards around his farm. She happened to be there on September 21, 2000. On that day, a tree branch fell on Richards's head and knocked him out.

17 Lulu quickly hopped back to Richards's house. She began banging on the door and barking like a dog.

18 Lulu was clearly trying to get the family's attention because, according to Richards's daughter Celeste, "she never acts like that."

19 Lulu barked for 15 minutes. At last, Celeste and her mother went outside. Lulu led them straight to Richards's body. Medical workers later said that if he hadn't been found so quickly, his head wounds could have killed him.

20 Lulu saved Richards's life. Yet other kangaroos have tried to kill people. So which is it? Are kangaroos our friends or our foes? Or is it possible they are a little bit of both? ❧

A Finding the Main Idea

One statement below tells the main idea of the article. One statement is too general, or too broad. The other statement explains only part of the article; it is too narrow. Label the statements using the following key:

M—Main Idea   B—Too Broad   N—Too Narrow

_____ 1. Kangaroos have attacked humans, but at times they have also proved themselves to be helpful friends. Dealing with them is a problem that must be solved in Australia.

_____ 2. Animals can be both friends and foes. People must find ways to handle animals in ways that are both kind to the animals and safe for humans.

_____ 3. A kangaroo attacked John Crouch and his wife, Helen. The attack was so fierce that Crouch had to kill the kangaroo to stop it from killing him and his wife.

Score 4 points for each correct answer.

_____ **Total Score:** Finding the Main Idea

B Recalling Facts

How well do you remember the facts in the article? Put an X in the box next to the answer that correctly completes each statement.

1. Sylvia Aldren was attacked by a kangaroo while she was

☐ a. teasing the animal.
☐ b. picking flowers.
☐ c. taking a picture of a baby kangaroo.

2. Pauline and Doug Lawton survived an attack by

☐ a. killing a kangaroo with an axe.
☐ b. calling their neighbors to drive a kangaroo away.
☐ c. scaring a kangaroo away by themselves.

3. During the 1900s,

☐ a. the number of kangaroos in Australia fell.
☐ b. kangaroos came to Australia.
☐ c. the Australian government agreed to let hunters and farmers kill up to 5.2 million kangaroos each year.

4. The kangaroo that Leonard Richards took in when it was a baby saved his life by

☐ a. carrying him to the hospital.
☐ b. getting his family's attention.
☐ c. fighting off another kangaroo.

Score 4 points for each correct answer.

_____ **Total Score:** Recalling Facts

C | Making Inferences

When you draw a conclusion that is not directly stated in the text, you are making an inference. Put an X in the box next to the statement that is a correct inference.

1.

☐ a. Kangaroos are large, strong animals.

☐ b. At top speed, kangaroos hop just about as fast as humans run.

☐ c. The weather in Australia is always cool and wet.

2.

☐ a. A kangaroo doesn't attack a person unless that person attacks it first.

☐ b. Kangaroos give up their attacks quickly as soon as the victim tries to fight back.

☐ c. In Australia, the government decides which animals can be killed and which should be protected.

> Score 4 points for each correct answer.
>
> _____ **Total Score:** Making Inferences

D | Using Words

Put an X in the box next to the definition below that is closest in meaning to the underlined word.

1. The workers were so <u>desperate</u> to escape the fire that they jumped from the third-floor window.

☐ a. bored; not interested

☐ b. almost hopeless and very fearful

☐ c. very happy; filled with joy

2. Many plants and animals have trouble finding water during <u>droughts</u>.

☐ a. months filled with warm, dry days and cool, wet nights

☐ b. times when a great deal of rain falls

☐ c. long times when no rain falls

3. One large pizza was <u>sufficient</u> to feed all of us. Two pizzas would have been too much.

☐ a. enough

☐ b. handy

☐ c. eager

4. Soon after we got a cat, the mouse <u>population</u> in our house went down to zero.

☐ a. the number of living things in a certain area

☐ b. a trap for catching animals that are not wanted

☐ c. anything that is famous or popular

5. The <u>humane</u> thing to do is to feed a hungry cat, not to shoo it away.

☐ a. cruel

☐ b. kind

☐ c. familiar

6. The <u>medical</u> report did not leave much hope that the patient would get better.

☐ a. of a government agency

☐ b. of the construction business

☐ c. of the practice of medicine

Score 4 points for each correct answer.

_____ **Total Score:** Using Words

E Author's Approach

Put an X in the box next to the correct answer.

1. Choose the statement below that is the weakest argument for protecting kangaroos in Australia.

☐ a. Some kinds of kangaroos are rare.

☐ b. Kangaroos are too cute to kill.

☐ c. Most kangaroos never hurt anyone.

2. Choose the statement below that best explains how the author deals with the opposite point of view.

☐ a. The author describes how kangaroos attacked Sylvia Aldren, Doug and Pauline Lawton, and John Crouch.

☐ b. The author gives examples of kangaroos who attacked humans and a kangaroo who saved a man's life.

☐ c. The author explains that kangaroos have been in Australia for 15 million years and that their numbers have been growing in recent years.

3. The author probably wrote this article in order to

☐ a. show how cruel people can be to animals.

☐ b. make readers want to visit Australia.

☐ c. tell readers about an interesting problem.

Score 4 points for each correct answer.

_____ **Total Score:** Author's Approach

F	**Summarizing and Paraphrasing**

Put an X in the box next to the correct answer.

1. Which summary says all the important things about the article?

☐ a. Although kangaroos have lived in Australia for 15 million years, they have become a problem only recently. Now the government says that they are only pests and lets millions of them be killed each year.

☐ b. Kangaroos have been attacking humans and eating crops in Australia, probably because there are too many kangaroos there. But many people still like kangaroos. Australians are divided on whether to kill or protect kangaroos.

☐ c. Leonard Richards and his family probably do not want any kangaroos killed. They believe that a kangaroo they named Lulu saved Richards's life after a heavy branch fell on his head and knocked him out.

2. Which sentence means the same thing as the following sentence? "Huge kangaroo packs roam the land."

☐ a. Kangaroos are traveling around Australia in big groups.

☐ b. Backpacks with kangaroos pictured on them are popular in Australia.

☐ c. Large kangaroos live in Australia.

Score 4 points for each correct answer.

_____ **Total Score:** Summarizing and Paraphrasing

G	**Critical Thinking**

Put an X in the box next to the correct answer.

1. Choose the statement below that states an opinion.

☐ a. Kangaroos are really cute and should be protected.
☐ b. Kangaroos can jump 30 feet in a single bounce.
☐ c. Kangaroos can hop at speeds of up to 50 miles per hour.

2. From information in the article, you can predict that

☐ a. the government will find it hard to please everyone.
☐ b. farmers will soon decide that they don't really want to kill any kangaroos.
☐ c. the people of Australia will decide that they don't want kangaroos anymore and will kill all of them.

3. Australian farmers and wildlife experts are different because

☐ a. only the wildlife experts really care about kangaroos and other animals.
☐ b. only the farmers are afraid of kangaroos and believe they should all be killed.
☐ c. the farmers want more kangaroos killed and the wildlife experts want fewer killed.

4. What was the effect of running water pipes across farmland in Australia?

☐ a. Kangaroos got hurt when they tried to break the pipes.
☐ b. Kangaroos got enough water and food to stay alive.
☐ c. Australia had to pass laws to end the killing of kangaroos.

5. In which paragraph did you find the information or details to answer question 4?

☐ a. paragraph 12

☐ b. paragraph 14

☐ c. paragraph 15

Score 4 points for each correct answer.

_____ **Total Score:** Critical Thinking

Enter your score for each activity. Add the scores together. Record your total score on the graph on page 115.

_____ Finding the Main Idea

_____ Recalling Facts

_____ Making Inferences

_____ Using Words

_____ Author's Approach

_____ Summarizing and Paraphrasing

_____ Critical Thinking

_____ **Total Score**

Personal Response

How do you think Sylvia Aldren felt when she saw the kangaroo staring at her?_____

_____

_____

Self-Assessment

One of the things I did best when reading this article was

_____

I believe I did this well because _____

_____

A Special Kind of Horse Power

Something was wrong. Pat Parelli and his wife didn't know what it was. But they knew that something was wrong with their infant son, Caton.

2   At first, doctors thought Caton had a vision problem. But when the boy was three months old, he slipped into a deep sleep called a *coma*. That's when doctors discovered the real problem. A virus had gotten into Caton's body, and it was causing his brain to swell. Doctors had to act quickly to save his life. But they feared Caton's brain had already been badly harmed.

3   "The doctors told us that if Caton lived through the night, he would probably never walk or talk," recalls Pat Parelli.

4   Caton did live. His parents brought him home from the hospital, hoping to make his life as ordinary as possible. For Pat, that meant being around horses, because Pat is a horse trainer. He has loved horses all his life. So when Caton was just six months old, Pat began taking him out for rides. "I'd snuggle him in

An eight-year-old boy who has cerebral palsy and autism takes a 30-minute ride on a horse as part of his treatment.

front of my saddle, and off we'd ride," recalls Pat. "Riding gave him a sense of rhythm and motion." In time, Caton learned to sit up straight in the saddle. He developed an excellent sense of balance. And in 1988, when he was five, he made a big leap forward.

5   "I saw that moment, like the light bulb going off," Pat says. "He got the idea he had to cause something to happen in his lower body to make the horse move forward." As Caton learned to control the horse, he learned to control his own body as well. Soon he could ride on his own. He could speak clearly too. "Something special had happened," says Pat. "And I knew the horse was responsible."

6   Pat is not the only one who has seen this happen. Europeans have been putting special-needs children on horses for many years. Now the word is spreading. Americans are discovering the healing power of horses.

7   For starters, riding a horse can help a child learn to sit or walk better. That's because a horse walks a bit like a human. Horses take the same number of steps each minute as humans take. And horses space their steps the same way we do. As horses move, their riders move too. The movement helps children understand what walking feels like. It helps them gain a sense of balance. And this movement builds the muscles children need for walking. Danielle Kern often works with special-needs children.

She says, "No machine has ever been invented to take the place of a horse's muscle groups' moving from side to side, forward and back, and up and down."

8 Riding strengthened Stormie Sanders's legs. Stormie suffered brain damage during birth, and she couldn't walk, talk, sit up, or see well. But after a few months of work on a horse, she had better control of her body. "We used to hold her up, and she'd fall back down," says her father. "Now she can stand on her own." Stormie also learned to say a word clearly. It is a word she uses when she is on her horse: "Go!"

9 Saara Duncan also made great progress on a horse. Saara had difficulty breathing. Her eyes were badly crossed, and one knee and hip didn't grow properly. But on a horse, she could leave these problems behind. By age three, she was able to sit on a horse and even stand up in the stirrups. Four adults walked at the front and the sides of the horse to encourage Saara and make sure she didn't fall off.

10 Many of the children who work with horses are deaf or blind. Blind children learn to lift their heads when riding. This helps them stand straighter. Deaf children learn to balance their bodies better.

11 And there is one more thing. Riding a horse lifts a child's spirits. It makes children feel better about themselves. "This is an animal that will accept them for what they are—black, white, beautiful, or ugly," says Ginny Elliott. Elliott works at a school for children who are deaf and blind. She says, "There is a bonding between the horse and the rider that gives the children a sense of freedom and adventure they can't get anywhere else."

12 Six-year-old Vojta Kares can't sit on a horse. He is too weak. Still, he can lie down on one. He rides on his stomach, facing backwards. Adults walk beside him as he and his horse slowly move along. Vojta can't talk. But his big smile lets everyone know he is having a good time.

13 The horses that work with these children must be specially chosen and trained. They need to be gentle. They must get used to noises and any sudden movements a child might make. In nature, horses will run if something strange happens. Here they must learn to stay put.

14 Children often become very attached to their horses. Bethany Lee knows all about that. Lee runs a riding program for special-needs children. She knows just how important the horses are to them. "Some have a picture of their horse on the wall," says Lee. "For countless kids, their first word was not *mama* but *giddy up* or the name of their horse!"

A | Finding the Main Idea

One statement below tells the main idea of the article. One statement is too general, or too broad. The other statement explains only part of the article; it is too narrow. Label the statements using the following key:

M—Main Idea   B—Too Broad   N—Too Narrow

_____ 1. Most people know that horses are useful to humans in many ways.

_____ 2. Riding a horse has proved to be a useful tool for helping special-needs children grow in body and spirit.

_____ 3. Riding a horse helped Caton Parelli develop control over his body after a virus hurt his brain.

Score 4 points for each correct answer.

_____ **Total Score:** Finding the Main Idea

B | Recalling Facts

How well do you remember the facts in the article? Put an X in the box next to the answer that correctly completes each statement.

1. Caton Parelli's problems were caused by

☐ a. a virus.
☐ b. trouble during birth.
☐ c. an accident.

2. Riding horses

☐ a. helps special-needs children read better.
☐ b. makes children fear big animals.
☐ c. helps children gain a sense of balance.

3. By the age of three, Saara Duncan could

☐ a. ride on a horse without any adults nearby.
☐ b. sit on a horse and stand in the stirrups.
☐ c. get on a horse without any help and ride away.

4. Horses that work with special-needs children are trained to

☐ a. run away fast when they hear loud noises.
☐ b. stay calm when something strange happens.
☐ c. stay perfectly still whenever a child is on their backs.

Score 4 points for each correct answer.

_____ **Total Score:** Recalling Facts

C | Making Inferences

When you draw a conclusion that is not directly stated in the text, you are making an inference. Put an X in the box next to the statement that is a correct inference.

1.

☐ a. Pat Parelli knew from the beginning that riding a horse would help his son learn how to speak.

☐ b. Pat Parelli has ridden a horse while holding his son many times over the years.

☐ c. Doctors are never wrong when they say what will happen in the future.

2.

☐ a. Adults who work with special-needs children must be careful and patient.

☐ b. Big changes usually happen within a few days after special-needs children begin riding horses.

☐ c. Riding horses sometimes makes blind children see better and deaf children hear better.

Score 4 points for each correct answer.

_____ **Total Score:** Making Inferences

D | Using Words

Put an X in the box next to the definition below that is closest in meaning to the underlined word.

1. When my grandfather was an infant, he slept in the dresser drawer for a few weeks.

☐ a. a young baby

☐ b. a tourist

☐ c. an adult

2. Because the movie was excellent, I went back to see it again.

☐ a. expensive

☐ b. awful

☐ c. very good

3. I want to thank whoever is responsible for planning this wonderful party.

☐ a. first in line

☐ b. deserving of thanks or blame

☐ c. not interested in doing something

4. The little girl's feet didn't reach the stirrups, so the stirrups had to be raised.

☐ a. flat-bottomed rings that hang from a saddle and are used to hold a rider's feet

☐ b. special shoes that are worn by people who ride horses

☐ c. people whose job it is to teach children how to ride horses

5. The <u>bonding</u> between the mother cat and her kittens begins when she starts to lick them clean.

☐ a. process of destroying
☐ b. process of pulling away from
☐ c. process of connecting

6. I have told you <u>countless</u> times to make your bed in the morning.

☐ a. fewer than zero
☐ b. too many to be counted
☐ c. referring to a time before numbers were invented

Score 4 points for each correct answer.

_____ **Total Score:** Using Words

E   Author's Approach

Put an X in the box next to the correct answer.

1. The main purpose of the first paragraph is to

☐ a. tell the reader that Caton Parelli had a problem.
☐ b. describe exactly what was wrong with Caton Parelli.
☐ c. compare Caton Parelli and his parents.

2. From the statements below, choose the one that you believe the author would agree with.

☐ a. Children with balance problems should stay away from large animals such as horses.
☐ b. Horses can be helpful and gentle with children.
☐ c. Letting Saara Duncan ride a horse was probably a bad idea.

3. What purpose does the author give in paragraph 6 for writing the article?

☐ a. to tell what is meant by the phrase *special-needs children*
☐ b. to make readers want to live in Europe because Euopeans ride horses more often than Americans ride them
☐ c. to tell readers that people in the United States are beginning to understand how horses can help children

---

Score 4 points for each correct answer.

_____ **Total Score:** Author's Approach

F | Summarizing and Paraphrasing

Put an X in the box next to the correct answer.

1. Which summary says all the important things about the article?

☐ a. Horses and humans walk in similar ways. Horses take the same number of steps each minute as humans take. Horses space their steps the same way humans do.

☐ b. Children who ride horses often develop friendships with the horses. Sometimes, the first word a child says is not *mama* but the name of his or her horse.

☐ c. Riding horses helps special-needs children develop their muscles and balance and can also lift their spirits. People who work with these children are now putting them on horses, with good results.

2. Which sentence means the same thing as the following sentence? "Europeans have been putting special-needs children on horses for many years."

☐ a. In Europe, everyone rides horses, including special-needs children.

☐ b. Europeans have understood for years that horses can help children with special needs.

☐ c. Children in Europe have special needs since they have been riding horses for many years.

Score 4 points for each correct answer.

_____ **Total Score:** Summarizing and Paraphrasing

G | Critical Thinking

Put an X in the box next to the correct answer.

1. Choose the statement below that states a fact.

☐ a. Pat Parelli took his son riding on horses when Caton was six months old.

☐ b. Holding an infant while riding on a horse is too dangerous and should not be allowed.

☐ c. More people should take their babies for rides on horses.

2. From information in the article, you can predict that

☐ a. the government will not allow special-needs children to ride horses in the future.

☐ b. more special-needs children will have the chance to ride horses in the future.

☐ c. horse lovers will soon stop parents from asking horses to carry special-needs children.

3. Caton Parelli and Stormie Sanders are alike because

☐ a. both were born with knee and hip problems.

☐ b. both had brain problems.

☐ c. both were born blind.

4. Which paragraphs provide information that supports your answer to question 3?

☐ a. paragraphs 2 and 8

☐ b. paragraphs 1, 2, 3, and 4

☐ c. paragraphs 8 and 9

5. If you were a teacher of special-needs children, how could you use the information in the article to help your students?

☐ a. I would ride a horse myself and tell my students what it feels like.

☐ b. I would have my students sit in a saddle and pretend they are on horses.

☐ c. I would find a way to let my students ride gentle horses.

Score 4 points for each correct answer.

_____ **Total Score:** Critical Thinking

Enter your score for each activity. Add the scores together. Record your total score on the graph on page 115.

_____ Finding the Main Idea

_____ Recalling Facts

_____ Making Inferences

_____ Using Words

_____ Author's Approach

_____ Summarizing and Paraphrasing

_____ Critical Thinking

_____ **Total Score**

Personal Response

I know how Ginny Elliott feels because _____

_____

Self-Assessment

I can't really understand how _____

_____

Don't Mess with the Gorilla

This photo of Max, a gorilla at the Johannesburg Zoo in South Africa, was taken on the day Max made his first appearance after being shot by a thief. Max's mate sits in the background by a tree.

According to the old saying, it's always best to "look before you leap." Isaac Mofokeng did not remember that advice—and he lived to regret it. On July 18, 1997, Mofokeng leaped over a small wall. He thought he was jumping to safety. But in fact, he ended up in a pen with a 500-pound gorilla.

2 Mofokeng's troubles began early that day. He planned to rob a house in Johannesburg, South Africa. He broke into the house at 9 A.M. But the owners saw him. They called the police. When the police came, Mofokeng took off. He ran into the city zoo. He hoped to hide there. But police followed him in. So Mofokeng ran up onto a raised viewing platform. This was where visitors went to look at gorillas. From the platform, people could look over a small wall and across a 15-foot ditch. They could see Max and Lisa. These were two mountain gorillas that lived in the zoo.

3 Unfortunately for Mofokeng, he did not know he was looking at the gorilla compound. All he knew was that he was still being chased by police. He later said he "jumped over the wall thinking I would be safe." Instead, he fell into the ditch and found himself trapped with the gorillas.

4 After Mofokeng landed in the ditch, he scrambled to his feet and headed through a door in the compound. It led to the "night room," where the gorillas slept.

That's when he came face to face with Max. "It's difficult to say who was the more surprised," said one zoo official.

5 Gorillas are gentle animals. They eat plants and fruit. They attack only if they think they are in danger. In this case, Max clearly felt threatened. A total stranger had just dropped into his home. So he did what came naturally: he attacked.

6 "I thought my last day had come," Mofokeng said. "The first thing the gorilla did was rip my jeans and bite me."

7 Max slammed Mofokeng into a wall. Mofokeng pulled out his gun. For a brief moment, he thought about shooting himself. "I thought it would be better to kill myself than be torn apart by the gorilla."

8 But he quickly changed his mind. He turned the gun toward Max and began shooting. One bullet hit the gorilla in the jaw. A second struck him in the left shoulder. Mofokeng later claimed he didn't really want to hurt Max. He said, "I was fighting for my life."

9 Just then, the police appeared. They had followed Mofokeng into the gorilla pen. An officer pointed his gun at Mofokeng. When Mofokeng didn't give himself up, the officer shot him in the leg. The officer then told Mofokeng to put down his gun. He told Mofokeng to run to the tunnel that workers used to bring Max food.

That way, Mofokeng could get away from the gorilla and be arrested by the police.

10   By this time, Max was crazy with fear and pain. Blood was pouring from his wounds. When Mofokeng ran toward the tunnel, Max followed him. Then Max turned on the police officers. He grabbed two of them, one under each arm. Max bit one of the officers. He broke the other one's arm.

11   At last, zoo workers were able to shoot Max with a dart. The dart contained medicine that put him to sleep. Mofokeng was taken away by police. In time, he and the police officers recovered from their injuries.

12   Meanwhile, zoo workers didn't know how to treat Max's wounds. They put him in the back of a pickup truck and rushed him to the hospital. Doctors wanted to put Max into a machine that would show all his injuries. But he was too big. He didn't fit into the machine. So they took simple X-rays. An X-ray is a ray that can go though skin to show the inside of a body. The X-rays showed that one bullet had gone clean through Max's body. The other was still embedded deep in his shoulder. The doctors decided it was best to leave it there.

13   It took a while, but Max got better. When he left the hospital, officials put a huge sign over the zoo entrance. It read: "Max Is Out!" Max then returned to his mate, Lisa, who had been badly scared by the shooting. For three days after the event, Lisa wouldn't eat a thing. And when Max returned, she followed him around more closely than she had ever done before.

14   Max and Lisa may not have known it, but Max was now famous. People called him a hero. Newspapers wrote many stories about him. An artist did a special painting of Max. Copies of it were sold to help raise money for the zoo. The zoo also sold Max T-shirts and posters. And fans from around the world sent him cards and letters.

15   Max didn't have to worry about seeing Isaac Mofokeng ever again. Mofokeng was sentenced to many years in prison for his crime.

A Finding the Main Idea

One statement below tells the main idea of the article. One statement is too general, or too broad. The other statement explains only part of the article; it is too narrow. Label the statements using the following key:

M—Main Idea   B—Too Broad   N—Too Narrow

_____ 1. When Isaac Mofokeng got to the Johannesburg Zoo, he ran up onto a raised platform. From that platform, visitors could view the two mountain gorillas, Max and Lisa.

_____ 2. Zoos are good places for viewing animals, such as gorillas, up close. Zoo workers do their best to take care of the animals and keep them safe and happy.

_____ 3. Some people call a gorilla named Max a hero for fighting a robber who broke into Max's pen. Max recovered from being shot by the robber, who went to jail.

Score 4 points for each correct answer.

_____ **Total Score:** Finding the Main Idea

B Recalling Facts

How well do you remember the facts in the article? Put an X in the box next to the answer that correctly completes each statement.

1. Isaac Mofokeng ran into Max and Lisa's compound

☐ a. in the morning.
☐ b. in the late afternoon.
☐ c. at night.

2. Mofokeng said he shot Max because

☐ a. he hates all animals.
☐ b. he hates all gorillas.
☐ c. he was afraid Max would kill him.

3. After shooting Mofokeng, an officer told the robber to put down his gun and

☐ a. jump back out of the compound.
☐ b. run to a tunnel.
☐ c. lie down and pretend to be dead.

4. One bullet from Mofokeng's gun

☐ a. went through Max's left foot.
☐ b. got stuck in Max's left leg.
☐ c. got stuck in Max's left shoulder.

Score 4 points for each correct answer.

_____ **Total Score:** Recalling Facts

C | Making Inferences

When you draw a conclusion that is not directly stated in the text, you are making an inference. Put an X in the box next to the statement that is a correct inference.

1.

☐ a. Isaac Mofokeng was a fast, fit man.

☐ b. Isaac Mofokeng cared more about animals than he cared about himself.

☐ c. If a gorilla is fighting a person, any other gorilla that lives with it helps out by fighting that person too.

2.

☐ a. If a person or an animal is shot, the only way to treat it is by removing the bullet.

☐ b. Max was much bigger and heavier than Mofokeng or the police officers.

☐ c. Planners of the Johannesburg Zoo expected people to jump into the gorillas' compound.

Score 4 points for each correct answer.

_____ **Total Score:** Making Inferences

D | Using Words

Put an X in the box next to the definition below that is closest in meaning to the underlined word.

1. My mother gave me good <u>advice</u> when she told me to save my money.

☐ a. a special dish cooked for a certain person

☐ b. a party to celebrate a special event

☐ c. an opinion about what to do

2. Now that it is raining, I <u>regret</u> that I didn't bring an umbrella.

☐ a. feel sorry

☐ b. feel happy

☐ c. feel relieved

3. The prisoner dreamed of being allowed to leave the <u>compound</u> someday.

☐ a. lunchroom or dining room

☐ b. place of business; company

☐ c. place to live surrounded by walls

4. The robbers were <u>arrested</u> by police as they left the bank with the money they had stolen.

☐ a. thanked for their fine work

☐ b. caught and taken to jail

☐ c. given a prize

5. The coin was <u>embedded</u> in the wet cement, and no one could get it out.

☐ a. put firmly into something
☐ b. lying on top of
☐ c. costing more than something else

6. To punish the robber for her <u>crime</u>, the judge sentenced her to six months in jail.

☐ a. an action taken to protect the law
☐ b. an action that breaks the law
☐ c. someone who breaks the law

Score 4 points for each correct answer.

_____ **Total Score:** Using Words

| **E** | **Author's Approach** |

Put an X in the box next to the correct answer.

1. What is the author's purpose in writing this article?

☐ a. to get the reader to give money to zoos
☐ b. to tell the reader about the ways that animals are treated when they are sick or hurt
☐ c. to describe what happened when someone ran into a zoo

2. From the statements below, choose the one that you believe the author would agree with.

☐ a. Mofokeng did the right thing when he shot Max to protect himself.
☐ b. People who think that Max was a hero are silly, and everyone should just stop talking about this event.
☐ c. It is easy to understand why Max acted as he did when Mofokeng dropped in on him.

3. The author tells this story mainly by

☐ a. describing events in the order they happened.
☐ b. comparing different topics.
☐ c. using his or her imagination.

Score 4 points for each correct answer.

_____ **Total Score:** Author's Approach

F | Summarizing and Paraphrasing

Put an X in the box next to the correct answer.

1. Which summary says all the important things about the article?

☐ a. Isaac Mofokeng had planned to rob a house in Johannesburg, South Africa. But when the owners of the house saw him, he ran to a nearby city zoo.

☐ b. Max, a gorilla in a zoo in South Africa, was surprised in his pen by a robber escaping from police. Max fought the robber until the police arrived. People around the world call Max a hero.

☐ c. Max and Lisa were mountain gorillas at a city zoo in Johannesburg, South Africa. When Max was taken to the hospital, his mate, Lisa, refused to eat for three days. When he came back, she followed him closely.

2. Which sentence means the same thing as the following sentence? "The X-rays showed that one bullet had gone clean through Max's body."

☐ a. The X-rays showed that one bullet had gone in one side of Max's body and gone out the other.

☐ b. According to the X-rays, one bullet had actually gone in and cleaned Max's body.

☐ c. The X-rays showed that one clean bullet had entered Max's body.

Score 4 points for each correct answer.

_____ **Total Score:** Summarizing and Paraphrasing

G | Critical Thinking

Put an X in the box next to the correct answer.

1. Choose the statement below that states an opinion.

☐ a. After Isaac Mofokeng left a house in Johannesburg, South Africa, he ran into the city zoo.

☐ b. Mofokeng shot the gorilla named Max at least twice—once in the jaw and once in the left shoulder.

☐ c. Zoo officials should make it harder to get inside the gorillas' compound.

2. Max and Mofokeng are alike because

☐ a. both recovered from injuries after a while.

☐ b. both became heroes.

☐ c. both were arrested by police.

3. The doctors could not use a special machine to find all the places where Max had been hurt. What was the cause of their problem?

☐ a. Max refused to get into the machine.

☐ b. Max was too big to fit into the machine.

☐ c. The hospital that owned the machine didn't want it to be used on a gorilla.

4. In which paragraph did you find the information or details to answer question 3?

☐ a. paragraph 10

☐ b. paragraph 12

☐ c. paragraph 13

5. Which lesson about life does this story teach?

☐ a. Even people who break the law love animals and will do anything to protect them.

☐ b. Humans are the only animals who become upset when things they don't expect happen.

☐ c. Animals, just like people, do not like to be surprised by strangers in their own home.

Score 4 points for each correct answer.

_____ **Total Score:** Critical Thinking

Enter your score for each activity. Add the scores together. Record your total score on the graph on page 115.

_____ Finding the Main Idea

_____ Recalling Facts

_____ Making Inferences

_____ Using Words

_____ Author's Approach

_____ Summarizing and Paraphrasing

_____ Critical Thinking

_____ **Total Score**

Personal Response

I know how it feels to _____

_____

Self-Assessment

When reading the article, I was having trouble with

_____

_____

Compare and Contrast

Pick two stories in Unit Three in which an animal made a big difference in someone's life.
Use information from the stories to fill in this chart.

Title	Who was helped or hurt by the animal in the story?	How did the animal help or hurt that person?	How does that person feel about the animal now?

Tell how an animal helped or hurt you or someone you know. _____

_____

_____

Comprehension and Critical Thinking Progress Graph

Directions: Write your score for each lesson in the box under the number of the lesson.
Then put a small X on the line directly above the number of the lesson and across from
the score you earned. Chart your progress by drawing a line to connect the Xs.

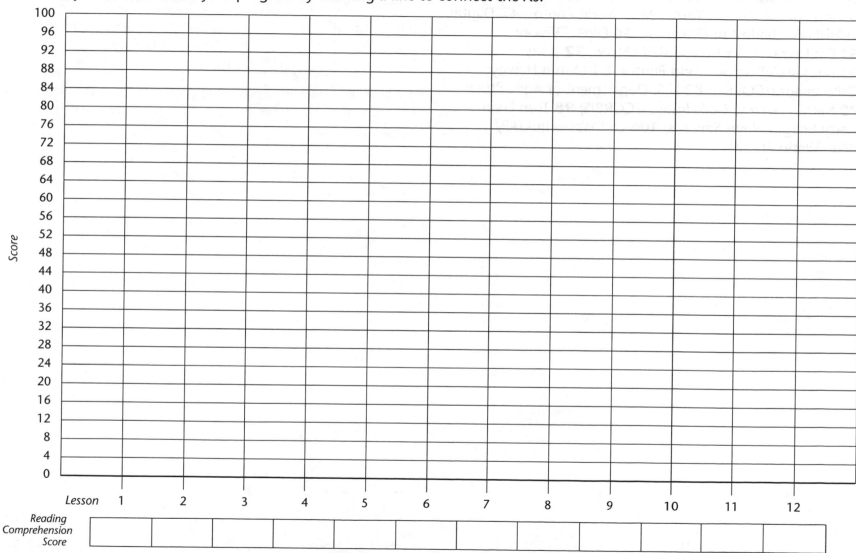

Photo Credits